# Florida
# FUN FACTS
## 2nd Edition

D1280524

Florida Tourists.

# *Florida*
# FUN FACTS

## *2nd Edition*

## Eliot Kleinberg

PINEAPPLE PRESS, INC.
Sarasota, Florida

Inquiries should be addressed to:
Pineapple Press, Inc.
P.O. Box 3889
Sarasota, Fl  34230

www.pineapplepress.com


Library of Congress Cataloging-in-Publication Data

Kleinberg, Eliot.
  Florida fun facts / Eliot Kleinberg.— 2nd ed.
     p. cm.
  Includes bibliographical references and index.
  ISBN 1-56164-320-3 (pb : alk. paper)
  1. Florida—Miscellanea.  I. Title.

  F311.5.K54 2004
  975.9'044—dc22                              2004019076


Second Edition
10  9  8  7  6  5  4  3  2  1

Design by Carol Tornatore
Printed and bound in the United States of America

# Contents

# Dedication

*This book is for all the pirates, smugglers, crooks, thieves,
opportunists, swindlers, suckers, slaves, masters, soldiers,
victims, hedonists, idealists, dreamers, lovers
and everyone else who, for better or worse,
has created the mosaic that will forever
be my home.*

# *Introduction*

**Q:** Why was this book produced?
**A:** Most Floridians these days are newcomers who know
nothing about this marvelous state or its storied past, which
is older and more colorful than that of any other state.
That's why this fun book was assembled: in order to
entertain and inform you about Florida in an interesting
and easy-to-read manner.

Florida is a historical contradiction of sorts. In many ways, the place
where Europeans first set foot on the continent is our youngest state. Until
this century, little of Florida below St. Augustine was populated, and Miami
was a village of a few thousand people.

There's something in Florida for lovers of every era: the ancient world of
the original Indian settlements; the sword and cross of Spanish colonization;
the swashbuckling period when pirates ruled the seas; the arrival of the
Americans, itching for opportunity; the tragedy of the Civil War and the
humiliation of Reconstruction; and the remarkable boom, unprecedented in
history, that, in a very short time, has transformed this land of swamps and
deserted beaches into America's vacation paradise.

The good, the bad, the proud, and the shameful combine for a patchwork
of the past that no other state can match for duration or variety.

**Q:** Will you enjoy this question-and-answer collection of
trivia about Florida?
**A:** We certainly hope so! In the process, we also hope you'll
learn a little bit about this wonderful state.

**Q:** What makes this book different from other Florida trivia books?
**A:** First, nearly every one of the 1,001 questions has been designed
to give even the novice an opportunity to take a stab at an answer.
We have come up with answers so entertaining you won't mind
getting stumped or caught off guard by the unexpected or obscure.

Most answers are followed by a sentence or two of explanation, so you won't be scratching your head and saying aloud, "Why is that?"

Second, the questions have been organized in chapters by subject and are accompanied by interesting and historic photographs.

Third, every entry has been checked against at least one source. An appendix at the back lists every question and its source or sources. We've also included a selected bibliography of books and other references to help you learn more about Florida.

And finally, an index in the back lets you look up selected topics directly.

**Q:** Are there any errors?
**A:** In a collection of this size, there is always the possibility of mistakes. And some entries are timely and therefore subject to change. Naturally, we're confident you won't find an inaccuracy. If you do, we invite you to bring it to our attention, along with corroboration of the proper information, and we'll make a correction in future editions. Write to us at the address on page 158.

*Eliot Kleinberg*

# 1
# *Strange Florida*

1. **Q:** Every April, people gather on either side of the Florida-Alabama line at Perdido Beach, near Pensacola, and throw what?
**A:** Mullets.

2. **Q:** What was a man arrested for doing topless in Palm Beach in 1979?
**A:** The shirtless male jogger was charged with violating the town's "topless" ordinance. An appeals court in Atlanta threw out the law in 1988.

3. **Q:** What did a storm deposit behind Molly Wilmot's Palm Beach oceanfront home November 23, 1984?
**A:** The 230-foot Venezuelan tanker *Mercedes I,* blown off course, beached behind a sea wall. It was stuck there for 103 days.

4. **Q:** What did visitors entering Florida near Pensacola in 1987 see that said "Welcome to Floirda"?
**A:** An official state highway sign. No one had noticed the mis-spelling until it was already up.

5. **Q:** What did one million official state maps place two blocks from its actual location in 1987?
**A:** They misplaced the state capitol complex in an inset of Tallahassee.

6. **Q:** In 1987, evangelist Oral Roberts—who said he would be killed by God unless he raised $8 million—was saved by $1.3 million from a Longwood dog track owner. Later, in an Orlando commercial, a man said he would die if he didn't sell 80,000 of what in the next month?
**A:** Tires. The man didn't die.

7. **Q:** In what kind of building is the police station in the tiny Panhandle town of Carrabelle?
**A:** A telephone booth. It's been called "The World's Smallest Police Station."

8. **Q:** What was unusual about a Jacksonville car wash that closed November 5, 1989?
**A:** It claimed to be America's only nude car wash.

9.  **Q:** In a bid to rid Sugarloaf Key of mosquitoes, a developer built a tower in 1929 to house what animal?
    **A:** Bats. The developer figured each bat could eat 3,000 mosquitoes. He spent $10,000 to build the 30-foot tower with a chute in the center to collect bat guano, which he planned to sell in 50-pound bags. But the tower never attracted any bats.

10. **Q:** What excuse did a woman use to successfully annul her Miami marriage on September 7, 1922?
    **A:** Although Prohibition was in effect, the woman said she was drunk the night of August 22 and did not realize she was in the middle of a wedding ceremony. She said she awakened the next morning in a West Palm Beach hotel and remembered she was engaged to someone else.

Artist Christo's pink islands adorn Biscayne Bay in May 1983. (*Miami News*)

11. **Q:** To whom did Eleanor McCaul ask a court to restrain her husband Thomas from visitation rights in their 1941 divorce?
    **A:** The Miami couple's dog. She said her husband had never supported the pet and had no right to see it.

12. **Q:** When West Palm Beach suffered three storms and three fires in its early life, numerologists in 1894 claimed to have found the cause in the town's name. What did they mean?
    **A:** It has 13 letters.

13. **Q:** What did eccentric artist Christo wrap in pink plastic in Biscayne Bay in May 1983?
    **A:** Eleven islands. The "surrounded islands" project used six million square feet of the stuff to give each island a 200-foot-wide ring. The project cost $3 million— $900,000 just for the material. Officials said it promoted tourism.

14. **Q:** What unusual mode of transportation did Julia St. Clair and her son use to get from Jacksonville to California between May 13, 1950, and June 25, 1951?
    **A:** They walked. The 2,500-mile, 13-month journey started with the woman pushing 135 pounds of food, clothing, and a cat in a wheelbarrow.

15. **Q:** What legacy of Sarasota circus magnate John Ringling led to a decades-long court battle?
    **A:** His body. When Ringling died of pneumonia in 1936, his body and that of his wife—who had died seven years earlier—were placed in temporary crypts in

New Jersey. Relatives squabbling over control of the Ringling estate could not decide where to put them permanently. In April 1987, they were secretly moved to unmarked crypts in an un-named southwest Florida cemetery. They were finally buried in

John and Mable Ringling

1991—by court order—at the museum grounds

**16. Q:** A strange creature called the Bardin Booger is said to roam the forests near Palatka. What is the Bardin Booger supposed to be?
**A:** A Florida version of Bigfoot.

**17. Q:** Who was Old Joe, whose murder August 1, 1966, in Wakulla Springs has never been solved?
**A:** A 650-pound, 11-foot, 2-inch alligator. The reptile had never molested people or pets. His stuffed body is in a glass case in the Wakulla Springs lodge.

**18. Q:** The Two-Toed Tom festival is held every fall in the tiny Panhandle town of Esto. Who was Toe-Toed Tom?
**A:** A legendary alligator.

**19. Q:** In the Panhandle town of Caryville, a festival revolves around the art of rotating a stick in the ground to make vibrations that raise what animal?
**A:** Worms; thus its name: the Worm Fiddling Festival.

**20. Q:** What famous film citizens were played by people based in Florida?
**A:** The Munchkins from *The Wizard of Oz*; they were circus performers at the Ringling Brothers winter home in Venice.

**21. Q:** What kind of play takes place every year in Lake Wales?
**A:** The Passion Play. The reenactment of the story of Jesus Christ plays during the Easter and Christmas seasons. The production, which moved to the Lake Wales Amphitheater from Pigeon Forge, Tenn., replaced the Black Hills Passion Play, which shut down in 1998 after nearly three decades in Florida.

**22. Q:** How does a penny turn into a dime in Wakulla Springs?
**A:** When dropped into the spring, as the penny falls, light patterns appear to change its color from copper to silver.

**23. Q:** What do boys dive into an inlet of the Gulf of Mexico to retrieve on Epiphany Day—January 6—in Tarpon Springs?
**A:** A cross. In the mostly Greek community north of St. Petersburg, the holiday—which commemorates the baptism of Jesus Christ—features a blessing of the fleet and the casting of a white cross. Whoever comes up with it is said to have good luck for a year.

24. **Q:** Whose statue will you find 20 feet underwater at John Pennekamp State Park in the upper Florida Keys?
    **A:** Jesus Christ. In 1990, atheists sued to have the 9-foot "Christ of the Deep" statue removed.

25. **Q:** In mock dog fights over the Florida Keys, what do U.S. Navy jets pose as?
    **A:** Russian MiG jets—complete with red stars—and other "bogies."

26. **Q:** Why did railroad workers dub the body of water north of Key Largo "Lake Surprise?"
    **A:** They thought it would be a cinch to build a causeway in the six feet of water until they learned the bottom was soft peat. It took 15 months to build a one-mile embankment.

27. **Q:** What part of Florida declared itself "The Conch Republic" in 1982?
    **A:** After a drug roadblock stopped traffic on U.S. 1, isolating the Keys, Key West declared its "independence," threw a giant party, and began a lucrative trade in "Conch Republic" souvenirs that continues to this day.

The Pirate Krewe sails into Tampa Bay to "seize" the city for the annual Gasparilla festival, an institution since 1904. (Florida News Bureau)

28. **Q:** What major Florida city is over-taken and captured by pirates once a year?
    **A:** Tampa. It's all part of the week-long Gasparilla festival which commemorates legendary pirate José Gaspár. The February festival began in 1904.

29. **Q:** What is "Fat Albert" and what is it doing nearly two miles above Cudjoe Key?
    **A:** The U.S. Air Force blimp, teth-ered to a 10,000-foot cable, sends information about suspected drug smuggling ships.

30. **Q:** Why is Orange (County) Lodge 36 in Apopka—which meets in Florida's oldest Masonic Lodge building—called a "moon lodge"?
    **A:** The group meets on or before the full moon and two weeks thereafter. The lodge was estab-lished in 1856 and the building constructed three years later.

31. **Q:** What fraternal organization settled the town of Moosehaven?
    **A:** Loyal Order of the Moose.

Since 1982, Key West residents have celebrated the indepen-dence of the "Conch Republic." (Florida Keys & Key West Visitors Bureau)

**32.** **Q:** True or false: Penney Farms was founded by the owner of the J.C. Penney stores.
**A:** True. Department store magnate J.C. Penney founded the community south of Jacksonville in 1927 for retired religious leaders.

**33.** **Q:** The small Panhandle town of Falmouth was named for a hunter's best friend. Can you identify the honoree?
**A:** The hunter's beloved dog.

**34.** **Q:** What is in the middle of Canova Drive in New Smyrna Beach?
**A:** The grave of the 16-year-old son of a citrus grower. The boy was killed in an 1860 hunting accident, and his father buried him there. The grave was never moved, so the street was built around it.

**35.** **Q:** Two railroad stops near Ocala are named for the star-crossed lovers of what famous play?
**A:** Romeo and Juliet. Townspeople decided on the names because of a similar incident involving two local lovers, but spelled the second town Juliette, for some reason lost to history.

**36.** **Q:** What vegetable's nickname is the name of a tiny community near Palatka in North Florida?
**A:** Spuds is in northeast Florida's potato-growing region.

**37.** **Q:** On the Apalachicola River, the wreck of the 150-foot steamer *Alice*, sunk in 1838, is socked in the mud. Its cargo may or may not remain. What was on board?
**A:** It held 180 60-gallon oak casks full of whiskey.

**38.** **Q:** In what unlikely vehicle did the U.S. Navy Training Center near landlocked Orlando specialize?
**A:** Submarines. Sailors trained in lakes in the navy's second largest boot camp. In 1993, a federal commission ordered it phased out.

**39.** **Q:** Why did Alabama and Georgia residents flock to convenience stores and service stations just inside Florida starting in 1988?
**A:** To buy lottery tickets. In the Florida Lottery's first 25 days, five of the top 10 sellers were in small border towns. Tops was a liquor store in Yulee, north of Jacksonville. Business dropped off after Georgia started its own lottery in June 1993.

**40.** **Q:** What did a man in the North Florida town of Luraville pull from the Suwannee River in 1979?
**A:** A 100-year-old, 10-ton, wood-burning train locomotive. Restaurant owner James Lancaster, 55, fulfilled a lifelong obsession when he recovered the engine, which locals believe fell while being loaded onto a barge in the 1890s. He spent $3,000 to have a 75-ton crane lift it out. He planned to restore the train and display it in front of his home.

**41.** **Q:** When imaginary explorers left a site east of Tampa in British author Jules Verne's book, where were they headed?
**A:** The fictional 19th-century astronauts were bound *From the Earth to the Moon*. NASA officials say Verne was right in placing his site between the equator and 28th parallel, to afford the best angle for a moon launch. Cape Canaveral is at latitude 28.5 degrees north. There is no evidence Verne visited Florida.

42. **Q:** In December 1945, a group of planes took off from a U.S. Navy air station in Fort Lauderdale and disappeared. What legend did the incident help start?
   **A:** The Bermuda Triangle.

43. **Q:** What happened to Eastern Airlines Flight 401 on approach to Miami International Airport on December 29, 1972?
   **A:** The airplane, loaded with holiday travelers, crashed into the Everglades. A total of 101 died. Some believe the remorseful ghost of the flight engineer later visited other Eastern planes, warning of equipment problems that would have led to crashes.

44. **Q:** Why would you be surprised to see Mr. Parker, manager of Sebring's Kenilworth Lodge at the front desk?
   **A:** He died in the 1950s. It is said his ghost still haunts the historic hotel; some staffers swear furniture, doors, and air conditioning knobs move, and taps are heard on doors from inside empty rooms.

45. **Q:** What guards the Indian and Banana Rivers in Melbourne?
   **A:** A 100-foot dragon, built in 1971 from a local legend that a dragon had chased away intruders. Glows and ghostly figures reportedly envelope it.

46. **Q:** What optical illusion can you see on Spook Hill in Lake Wales?
   **A:** Cars inexplicably appear to roll uphill.

47. **Q:** What Eastern religion's ancient temple stands on the campus of Florida Southern College in Lakeland?

**A:** When a missionary successfully converted an entire group of Hindus to Christianity, they gave him their old temple, which he shipped to Florida.

48. **Q:** When a religious group settled at the turn of the century in Estero, south of Fort Myers, the 200 members planned a "New Jerusalem" with how many residents?
   **A:** Ten million. The group believed we live inside the earth, not on it. When the leader died, followers waited in vain for him to return to life. They finally disbanded. The area is now a state historic site.

49. **Q**: What's the strange occupation of most residents of Cassadaga?
   **A:** The town of about 350 west of Daytona Beach, founded by a spiritualist leader in the 19th century, is home to 30 to 50 mediums, fortune tellers, and spiritual healers.

50. **Q:** According to one of several legends compiled by Florida State University professor J. Russell Reaver over four decades, what does Lake Mystic, near Tallahassee, lack?
   **A:** A bottom.

51. **Q:** According to legend, a horseman missing what body part rides the trail every midnight near Canoe Creek in Osceola County?
   **A:** His head. The story says a pioneer on a white horse was confronted by Spanish soldiers at the bridge across Canoe Creek. They took him to an oak tree, now called "Deadman's Oak," and beheaded him. It is said he now rides on his horse, searching for his head.

**52. Q:** According to legend, a peace treaty between Seminoles and what animals continues in effect to this day?
**A:** Snakes.

**53. Q:** A Spanish sailor chasing an Indian woman got caught in a tree, and when he died, his body wasted away, leaving only his beard? That legend supposedly explains what Florida vegetation?
**A:** The Spanish moss that hangs from trees everywhere.

**54. Q:** Why have people been baffled by Edward Leedskalnin's construction of Coral Castle near Homestead, with 1,100 tons of coral, some pieces weighing 30 tons?
**A:** Because the 5-foot, 100-pound Latvian immigrant used only handmade pulleys and levers salvaged from junkyards to lift and position the massive pieces himself. How he did it is still a mystery. The place is now a tourist attraction.

**55. Q:** What did parishioners at St. Nicholas Cathedral in Tarpon Springs claim to have seen a statue do in 1989?
**A:** Weep. Drops of moisture were reportedly seen around the halo and on the cheeks of Saint Nicholas, patron saint of sailors and children, in the heavily Greek town north of St. Petersburg.

# 2
# *Superlatives and Firsts*

1.  **Q:** What is Florida's most populous county?
    **A:** The Miami area's Dade County had 2.35 million people as of 2003.

2.  **Q:** What's Florida's least populated county?
    **A:** Tiny Lafayette County, in Florida's "Big Bend," halfway between Tallahassee and Gainesville. Its 7,057 residents (as of 2002) could fit comfortably into many high school football stadiums. Liberty County in the Panhandle, formerly the smallest, has 7,132, but is the most sparsely populated, with only nine people per habitable square mile.

3.  **Q:** What's the most densely populated county?
    **A:** Pinellas. The peninsular county is home to St. Petersburg, Clearwater, and a host of suburban and beach resort towns and packs 3,317 people per habitable square mile. Miami's Dade County has only a third the density—1,176 people per habitable square mile.

4.  **Q:** What's Florida's largest county in area, including water?
    **A:** Palm Beach County; at 2,578 square miles, it's half the size of Connecticut. The dimensions figure in the county's share of Lake Okeechobee.

5.  **Q:** What's Florida's smallest county in area?
    **A:** Tiny Union County, southwest of Jacksonville in North Florida, has only 245 square miles, including bodies of water. It could fit into Lake Okeechobee three times.

6.  **Q:** What Florida county added the most total residents between 1980 and 2000?
    **A:** Broward increased by 367,487 residents, an amount almost double that of Fort Lauderdale, its largest city and county seat, with 167,000. Its larger neighbor, Miami-Dade County, was second with 316,168.

7.  **Q:** What small North Florida county experienced a 163 percent population increase between 1980 and 1990, highest in the state?
    **A:** Flagler County, north of Daytona Beach. It was the highest again between 1990 and 2000, with a 73.6 percent increase.

8.  **Q:** What's Florida's wealthiest county?
    **A:** As of 2000, it's Palm Beach, with a per capita personal income

of 41,007. St. Augustine's St. Johns County is second, with $60,635. Palm Beach's northern neighbor, Martin, is third with 40,186. Naples' Collier County rounds out the "$40,000" club with $40,121.

9. **Q:** What lofty distinction does the Panhandle town of Lakewood hold?
   **A:** It's the highest point in flat Florida—a nose-bleeding 345 feet above sea level.

10. **Q:** What's higher: Florida's highest point or the Dade County Courthouse?
    **A:** The Panhandle town of Lakewood is 345 feet above sea level. Miami's Dade County Courthouse is 357 feet above the street, which is all of 20 feet above sea level.

11. **Q:** Which is higher: Florida's highest point or Colorado's lowest point?
    **A:** Florida's highest point—345 feet above sea level in the Panhandle town of Lakewood—is lower than the lowest points of 16 states: Colorado (3,350), Wyoming (3,026), New Mexico (2,817), Utah (2,000), Montana (1,800), South Dakota (962), Nebraska (840), North Dakota (750), Idaho (710), Kansas (680), Minnesota (602), Wisconsin (581), Michigan (572), Iowa (480), Nevada (470), and Ohio (433).

12. **Q:** What's Florida's largest lake?
    **A:** Lake Okeechobee. It's more than 700 square miles.

13. **Q:** Where's Florida's largest island?
    **A:** Merritt Island, in Brevard County, encompasses about 25,945 acres, or about 40-1/2 square miles.

14. **Q:** What's Florida's longest canal?
    **A:** The Miami Canal. It's 81 miles long, from Lake Okeechobee to Miami.

15. **Q:** Where is Florida's biggest springs?
    **A:** Silver Springs in Marion County, with an average flow of 823 cubic feet per second.

16. **Q:** Where's Florida's largest forest?
    **A:** The Apalachicola National Forest covers 557,000 acres, or more than 870 square miles. It's nearly three-fourths the size of Rhode Island. Most of the forest is pine hardwood.

17. **Q:** Which state park covers the most land area?
    **A:** It's Myakka River State Park in Sarasota County, with 28,875 acres, or more than 45 square miles. John Pennekamp State Park has 56,000 acres, but all but 2,340 acres is under water.

18. **Q:** What natural phenomenon extends 125 miles from Key West to just north of Elliott Key off Miami and is Florida's longest of its kind?
    **A:** A coral reef.

Lake Okeechobee is Florida's largest. (*Miami News*)

**19. Q:** In what city's downtown area is Florida's tallest building?
**A:** The 70-story Four Seasons Hotel and Tower in downtown Miami opened in the fall of 2003, dethroning the 55-story building which opened in October 1984 as the Southeast Bank building and is now the Wachovia building.

**20. Q:** In the town of Ochopee along U.S. 41 in Collier County, you'll find a building that's the smallest facility of its kind in America. What is it?
**A:** A post office. It's 8 feet, 4 inches by 7 feet, 3 inches and 10 feet 6 inches high—about the size of a garden shed.

The tiny post office in Ochopee, in the western Everglades, is the smallest in America.

**21. Q:** Where in Florida will you find the world's largest scientific building?
**A:** It's the Vehicle Assembly Building at Complex 39 at the John F. Kennedy Space Center in Cape Canaveral. It's 716 feet long, 518 feet wide, and 525 feet high. The building contains four bays, each with its own door 460 feet high. They're the world's largest doors.

**22. Q:** Where in Florida will you find the oldest known building in the Western Hemisphere?
**A:** In North Miami Beach. The Cloisters of the Monastery of St. Bernard, shipped to Florida in 1925 by publisher William Randolph Hearst, were built in Segovia, Spain, in 1141 A.D. They were assembled at their present site in 1954.

**23. Q:** What superlative is claimed by Tampa's Columbia restaurant?

Tampa's Columbia claims to be America's oldest and largest Spanish restaurant. (*Miami News*)

**A:** It is believed to be the oldest and largest Spanish restaurant in the United States.

**24. Q:** What world distinction does Tampa's 6-1/2-mile-long Bayshore Boulevard claim?
**A:** World's longest continuous sidewalk.

Bayshore Boulevard claims to be the world's longest sidewalk. (*Miami News*)

25. **Q:** What Florida town claims to have the longest pier on the Gulf of Mexico?
    **A:** Panama City Beach. The pier, built in 1978, extends 1,642 feet—about a third of a mile—into the Gulf.

26. **Q:** Where's the world's largest flowing well?
    **A:** Wekiva Falls' "Big Well," north of Orlando. It pumps 72 million gallons of water a day — almost enough for every person in Florida to flush the toilet once.

27. **Q:** Rushing water was measured on April 11, 1973, at a record-breaking rate of 14,325 gallons—enough to fill an average-sized South Florida pool—in one second. From where did it spout?
    **A:** Wakulla Springs, one of the largest and deepest in the world.

28. **Q:** What Florida town claims to have "the world's most beautiful beach"?
    **A:** Panama City Beach.

29. **Q:** Where will you find the world's longest conga line?
    **A:** At Miami's Calle Ocho festival. The massive street party on S.W. 8th Street, in the heart of the Cuban community, features the conga, or congo, a Latin line dance. A line made of 119,986 people dancing on March 13, 1988, made the *Guinness Book of World Records*.

30. **Q:** How tall is Florida's biggest sabal palm?
    **A:** The tallest version of the state tree was found in Highland Hammocks State Park, near Sebring, when the park was bought from private landowners in 1927. It is 90 feet tall.

31. **Q:** A marine monster weighing a half ton, nabbed off Pensacola, was the largest of what animal ever caught?
    **A:** Shark. The 1,065-pound tiger shark was caught in 1981. The heaviest red snapper—46 pounds, 8 ounces—was caught off Destin in October 1985. The biggest sailfish, weighing 116 pounds, was caught near Miami Beach in 1986.

32. **Q:** A 20-pound, 2-ouncer was the largest of what popular freshwater fish ever caught in Florida?
    **A:** The biggest largemouth bass—the state freshwater fish—was caught in May 1923 on the appropriately named Big Fish Lake in Pasco County. It is unofficial because the fish wasn't examined. The official record is a 17-1/4-pounder caught in Polk County on July 6, 1986.

33. **Q:** What world-record-setting item did Lorenzo Amato cook and cut into 94,248 slices in October 1987?
    **A:** A pizza. The pie—100 feet, 1 inch in diameter—was consumed by 30,000 spectators in Havana, near Tallahassee. Amato's record lasted only three years; a pizza created in Norwood, South Africa, measured 122 feet across.

34. **Q:** What culinary state record-holder stretched 736 feet?
    **A:** Florida's biggest spaghetti noodle was made at the Pampered Palate store in Boca Raton's Town Center mall in March 1986.

35. **Q:** The March 1986 Sertoma Club Barbecue in New Port Richey tied a world's record for consumption of what food?
    **A:** A filling 21,112 pounds of barbecued beef—more than 10-1/2 tons.

36. **Q:** A conglomeration weighing nearly 29 tons, prepared in a 13,000-gallon bowl, was the largest

of what menu item in Florida history?

**A:** Florida's biggest salad, weighing 57,685 pounds, was tossed in 1983 in Belle Glade, which bills itself as the world's winter vegetable capital. The world's record is a 57-1/2-ton (114,885-pound) salad made in California.

37. **Q:** What state-record-holding food item took 1,600 pounds of flour, 50 pounds of yeast and 20 pounds of sugar, and came out of the oven weighing 1,800 pounds?
    **A:** Florida's biggest pretzel was baked in 1987 for the South Florida Fair in West Palm Beach.

38. **Q:** What trademark Florida dessert item measuring 15 feet, 7 inches across and weighing more than a ton set a world size record?
    **A:** The world's largest key lime pie, made at the South Seas Plantation resort on Captiva Island in September 1987, weighed 2,138 pounds. Pies created at the state capitol in Tallahassee in 1989 and in Key West in 1997 claimed to be the largest, but they were only seven feet across.

39. **Q:** What religious ceremony in St. Augustine in 1565 was the first of its kind in the "New World?"
    **A:** Father Francisco Lopez de Mendoza Grajales offered the first Mass at North America's first mission, called "Nombre de Dios"— "Name of God."

40. **Q:** The beach at Siesta Key, in Sarasota, won what world superlative in 1989?
    **A:** Best beach. In a competition with 29 other beaches, it was declared to have the world's whitest and finest-textured beach sand.

41. **Q:** On February 27, 1987, two divers in North Florida broke a depth record for what kind of dive?
    **A:** It was the deepest dive ever into a cave. Using underwater scooters, the two descended 7,685 feet—nearly a mile and a half— into a cave at Manatee Springs, west of Gainesville. The dive took two hours, 40 minutes, followed by six hours of decompression to remove nitrogen that builds up in the bloodstream during long and deep dives.

42. **Q:** Archaeologists have uncovered the 200-year-old remains of Fort Mose, believed to be the first settlement in North America of what minority?
    **A:** Blacks. The fort, near St. Augustine, was a refuge for runaway slaves more than a century before Abraham Lincoln's Emancipation Proclamation.

43. **Q:** A mule-pulled setup was the first of what mode of transportation in Florida?
    **A:** Florida's first railroad, stretching all of eight miles, opened April 14, 1836, between St. Joseph Bay, on the Gulf of Mexico, and Lake Wimico, along the Apalachicola River.

44. **Q:** In what city did Florida's first phone exchange open on May 24, 1880?
    **A:** Jacksonville.

45. **Q:** What substance was found deep under the Sunniland field in northern Collier County on September 26, 1906?
    **A:** Oil. It was Florida's first oil well.

**46. Q:** What mode of transportation operated commercially for the first time in a trip from Tampa to St. Petersburg on January 1, 1914?
**A:** The world's first scheduled commercial airline flight crossed Tampa Bay.

**47. Q:** What kind of citrus was first developed in Manatee County in 1914?
**A:** The world's first pink grapefruits were discovered in a Palmetto nursery. Mutations were found on a branch.

**48. Q:** What speed did a car travel for the first time ever on March 29, 1927, at Daytona Beach?
**A:** Two hundred miles per hour.

**49. Q:** In what city did Florida's first television station go on the air March 21, 1949?
**A:** It was Miami's WTVJ-TV. About three months later, on June 10, 1949, the station was picked up

A diver enjoys the sights of John Pennekamp State Park, the nation's first underwater park. (*Miami News*)

on a set in an appliance store in Easton, Pa., 1,200 miles away. The bizarre phenomenon was blamed on an atmospheric glitch.

**50. Q:** What kind of college, founded in 1958 in St. Petersburg, was the first of its kind in the country?
**A:** A clown college.

**51. Q:** On March 15, 1960, John Pennekamp State Park was made the nation's first park with what distinction?
**A:** It was the first underwater park.

**52. Q:** On November 14, 1969, Richard Nixon became the first U.S. president to view what?
**A:** A space launch. He watched the liftoff of Apollo 12.

**53. Q:** On September 26, 1985, at Sea World, near Orlando, Baby Shamu became the first of what animal in known history to be born and thrive in captivity?
**A:** Killer whale.

A young Ralph Renick, who would become the dean of Florida news anchors, stands in front of the fledgling WTVJ-TV. (Wometco)

# 3

# *What's in a Name?*

1.  **Q:** What's the most popular word found in Florida city names?
    **A:** Not surprisingly, it's "Beach." According to the state's official highway map, 52 towns or cities contain the word. Second is "City" with 28, followed by "Springs" with 24, "Park" with 20, and "Fort" and "Palm," each with 12.

2.  **Q:** Of towns with multiple-word names, what word do most start with?
    **A:** Seventeen towns start with "Lake." The words "Fort" and "Saint" tie for second with 12, and "Port" has nine.

3.  **Q:** For which tree are the most Florida towns named?
    **A:** The palm: Palm Bay, Palm Beach, Palm Beach Gardens, Palm Beach Shores, Palm Coast, Palm Harbor, Palm Springs, Palmdale, Palmetto, Royal Palm Beach, South Palm Beach, West Palm Beach. Other greenery: Cypress, Floral City, Garden City, Grove Park, Groveland, Hawthorne, Holly Hill, Hollywood, Jasper, Lake Fern, Lantana, Laurel, Laurel Hill, Live Oak, Longwood, Melrose, Mossy Head, Mulberry, Oak Hill, Oakland, Oakland Park, Orchid, Pine Castle, Pinetta, Piney Point, Pineland, Plant City, Plantation, Poinciana, Roseland, Shady Grove, Shamrock, Walnut Hill, Westwood Lake, Wildwood, Winter Garden, and Zellwood.

4.  **Q:** For which fruit are most Florida towns named?
    **A:** The orange, of course: Orange City, Orange Heights, Orange Lake, Orange Park, Orange Springs, Port Orange. Others that belong in the kitchen: Cherry Lake, Citrus Park, Citrus Springs, Cocoa, Cocoa Beach, Coconut Creek, Cooks Hammock, Fruitland Park, Salt Springs, Sweet Gum Head, and Tangerine.

5.  **Q:** Which type of animal are the most Florida towns named for?
    **A:** Birds: Crows Bluff, Eagle Lake, Flamingo, Flamingo Bay, Osprey, Owl's Head. Mammals are second: Deer Park, Deerfield Beach, Elkton, Otter Creek, and Port Manatee. Fish have only Pompano Beach and Tarpon Springs.

6.  **Q:** Where in Florida can you find a baker, a barber, a cook, and a doctor?
    **A:** On the state map: the towns of Baker, Barberville, Cooks Hammock, and Doctors Inlet.

7.  **Q:** What three Panhandle cities' names link them to Latin America?
    **A:** Mexico Beach, Havana, and Panama City.

8.  **Q:** Was Panama City named for its Central American counterpart?
    **A:** Yes. Founders wanted to stress its location, on a straight line between Chicago and the Panama Canal.

9.  **Q:** For which foreign country's towns were the most Florida cities apparently named?
    **A:** The United Kingdom, with five: Oxford, Dover, Brighton, Inverness and Dundee. Many Florida towns were named by immigrants for their homelands, others by developers looking for exotic names. Some of the others: Hague (Netherlands); Oslo (Norway); Boulogne, Clermont (France); Geneva (Switzerland); Odessa, St. Petersburg (Russia); Venice (Italy); Andalusia, Seville (Spain); Arcadia (Greece); Panama City (Panama); Havana (Cuba); Freeport (Bahamas); Bagdad (Baghdad, Iraq); Melbourne (Australia); and Sumatra (Indonesia).

10. **Q:** What do the major American cities of Cleveland, Dallas, Raleigh, San Antonio, Hollywood, Oakland, and Memphis have in common?
    **A:** They have namesakes in Florida. Others: Gulfport and Vicksburg (Miss.), Youngstown (Ohio), Brownsville (Texas), Greensboro (N.C.), Greenville (Miss., S.C., N.C., Texas), Greenwood (Miss., S.C.), Gretna (La.), Wausau (Wis.), and Valparaiso (Ind.)

11. **Q:** For what part of America are the most Florida towns apparently named?
    **A:** The Northeast, to which many Floridians trace their roots: Plymouth, Quincy, Springfield (Mass.); Salem, Concord (Mass., N.H.); Portland (Maine); Bridgeport (Conn.); Bristol (Conn., R.I.); Providence (R.I.); Harlem, Lake Placid, Monticello (N.Y.); Watertown (Conn., Mass., N.Y.); Altoona (Pa.); Georgetown (Washington, D.C.); Princeton and Trenton (N.J.).

12. **Q:** Which four Florida town names reflect figures of Greek and Roman mythology?
    **A:** Jupiter, Neptune Beach, Juno Beach, and Apollo Beach.

13. **Q:** What small central Florida town's post office gets numerous requests for postmarks in December of every year?
    **A:** Christmas.

14. **Q:** Why did developers give Florida towns names like Frostproof, Mt. Pleasant and Winter Haven?
    **A:** The smart salesmen wanted hypnotic inducements to "Come on down!" Others: Concord, Enterprise, Fellowship, Fountain, Freeport, Land O' Lakes, Leisure City, New Harmony, New Hope, New Point Comfort, Niceville, Panacea, Safety Harbor, Sun City, and Treasure Island.

15. **Q:** Which season appears in most Florida town names?
    **A:** Winter, of course! Freezing

northerners would love to winter in Winter Beach, Winter Garden, Winter Haven, Winter Park, and Winter Springs. Other names that sound like they belong in a calendar: Century, Christmas, Day, Holiday, June Park, Spring Lake, Summerfield, and Sunrise.

16. **Q:** What three American Revolution themes became names of Florida counties?
    **A:** Liberty, Union, and Columbia.

17. **Q:** What do presidents Adams, Buchanan, Cleveland, Grant, Jackson, Monroe, Pierce, and Polk have in common in Florida?
    **A:** Fifteen towns or counties contain the names of those eight presidents, whether intentional or otherwise.

18. **Q:** How many Florida cities contain the word "Lincoln"?
    **A:** In this former Confederate state, there are none honoring the Yankee president.

19. **Q:** What counties are named for presidents?
    **A:** Washington, Jefferson, Madison, and Polk.

20. **Q:** What explorer has two counties named for him?
    **A:** Hernando de Soto.

21. **Q:** Why was present-day Hernando County renamed Benton County, then changed back?

Spanish explorer Hernando de Soto has two counties named for him.

**A:** It was named for explorer Hernando de Soto in 1843, then changed to Benton the following year to honor Missouri U.S. Sen. Thomas Hart Benton's support of Indian reoccupation. It was changed back by irate extremists in 1850 because of Benton's moderation on the Missouri Compromise, which had forbidden slavery west of the Mississippi and north of Missouri's southern border.

22. **Q:** What do American Revolution figures Benjamin Franklin, Alexander Hamilton, Marquis de Lafayette, and Francis "Swamp Fox" Marion have in common?
    **A:** All had Florida counties named for them.

23. **Q:** The Seminole Wars are memorialized in what county names?
    **A:** Seminole; Osceola for the warrior; Dade for Maj. Francis Dade, massacred in 1835 along with more than 100 troops in the Second Seminole War; Taylor for President Zachary Taylor, who led many U.S. troops during that war; and Jackson, for President Andrew Jackson, who first pursued the Seminoles in the First Seminole War.

24. **Q:** The Civil War era is the source for what Florida county names?
    **A:** Dixie was named for the Confederacy; Calhoun for South Carolina U.S. senator and states rights activist John C. Calhoun; Lee for Confederate Gen. Robert E. Lee; and Baker for Confederate state senator James McNair Baker.

25. **Q:** Whether intentional or otherwise, 13 towns and seven counties carry the names of people who held what Florida office?

**A:** They were colonial, territorial, or state governors, ranging from Juan Ponce de León (1513) to Bob Graham (1979-1987).

26. **Q:** How many counties have county seats with the same name?
**A:** Three: Madison, Sarasota, and Okeechobee. Palm Beach comes close: the island town's larger neighbor, West Palm Beach, is the county seat.

27. **Q:** Which counties are named for bodies of water?
**A:** Bay, Gulf, and Lake.

28. **Q:** How many counties have "saint" in their name?
**A:** Two—St. Johns and St. Lucie— plus Santa Rosa (Santa is Spanish for Saint).

29. **Q:** What county name is also a woman's first name?
**A:** Charlotte.

30. **Q:** What is the only county named for an animal?
**A:** Manatee.

31. **Q:** What counties are named for Florida's biggest crop?
**A:** Citrus and Orange.

32. **Q:** What's wrong with Citrus County's name?
**A:** The county north of Tampa really has no citrus. The industry flourished in the 1880s, when the county was established, but a series of hard freezes over the next decade wiped out the groves and drove growers south.

33. **Q:** What ever happened to Bloxham County and Call County?
**A:** They never happened. The name "Bloxham" was rejected by voters. The name "Call" was vetoed by the governor, and the county was later named Brevard.

34. **Q:** A Florida county and America's last land annexation on the North American continent are named for the same man. Who?
**A:** James Gadsden, an aide to Gen. Andrew Jackson during the 1818 Florida Indian campaign, is more famous for the 1853 Gadsden Purchase of a small area of modern-day New Mexico and Arizona.

35. **Q:** Counties in North Florida and New York's Long Island and an island in the Bahamas are named for what defunct European territory?
**A:** The former Duchy of Nassau, near present-day Wiesbaden, Germany.

36. **Q:** Alachua County may have been named for the Indian word for "jug." Why?
**A:** Historians say it may have referred to a large sinkhole near Gainesville.

37. **Q:** What unenviable distinction got a county named for Capt. Richard C. Bradford?
**A:** The county north of Gainesville was named for the first Confederate officer from Florida to be killed in the Civil War. Bradford, of Madison, died October 9, 1861, during the Battle of Santa Rosa Island, a Confederate attempt to take Fort Pickens, near Pensacola.

38. **Q:** What county was almost called Pinckney County?
**A:** Dade. In 1835, as the Florida legislature was preparing to name the Miami-area county Pinckney, word came that Major Francis Dade and his troops had been massacred by Seminoles.

David Levy (Florida Department of Natural Resources)

**39. Q:** What Florida county is named for a Jew?
**A:** Levy County is named for David Levy, the state's first U.S. senator and the first Jew in the nation to hold that post. Levy later had his surname changed to Yulee, and a town near Jacksonville bears that name.

**40. Q:** What Florida fort, and later city, was named for a Jew?
**A:** Fort Myers, named for Gen. Abraham C. Myers.

**41. Q:** Lake Worth, Florida, and Fort Worth, Texas, are named for whom?
**A:** Maj. Gen. William Jenkins Worth, leader in the Second Seminole War in Florida and the Mexican-American War in Texas and Mexico.

Maj. Gen. William Jenkins Worth led troops in Seminole and Mexican wars. (Library of Congress)

**42. Q:** For whom did pioneer F.A. Hendry, for whom Hendry County is named, name the town of LaBelle?
**A:** His daughters, Laura and Belle.

**43. Q:** Was Chiefland named for a chief?
**A:** Yes: a Creek chief who settled in the North Florida town after the Second Seminole War.

**44. Q:** Why was the town of Tequesta, in northern Palm Beach County, named for the wrong Indians?
**A:** The Tequesta lived down in the area of what is now Miami, but the developer liked the name; even after local historians explained the mixup, he wouldn't budge.

**45. Q:** How did Hobe Sound and Jupiter get their names from the same source?
**A:** Local Indians first called the Jupiter area "Hobe," pronounced HO-bay. Spaniards thought they were saying "Jove"—pronounced HO-vay—the Spanish pronunciation of a Roman name for the Greek god Zeus. The British preferred Jove's more common name: Jupiter.

**46. Q:** How did a town get a name like "Boca Raton," Spanish for "mouth of the mouse"?
**A:** Many thought it was because the inlet is shaped like a mouse's mouth or because sailors were referring to sharp, dangerous rocks. Historians say the real Boca Raton was a dangerous inlet at Miami Beach, and a mapmaker inadvertently placed it where it is now.

**47. Q:** What Palm Beach County lake was originally called Hypoluxo, which means "water all around, can't get out"?
**A:** Lake Worth. Before inlets were dug, the body of water separating Palm Beach and West Palm Beach was completely closed in. Now it's part of the Intracoastal Waterway.

**48. Q:** What South Florida town's name was shortened from Opatishawockalocka?
**A:** Opa-locka. The long word is Seminole for either a swamp or a big island covered by many trees and a swamp.

**49. Q:** What town boasted a famous mulberry tree?
**A:** Mulberry, of course. The tree marked a freight collection point for four major phosphate plants, and a railroad station was built on the spot, leading to settlement of the town. The tree reportedly weathered many powerful storms, some lightning strikes, and perhaps some lynchings. When it appeared to have died, townsfolk said it was for shame. When it one day sprouted new greenery, people said it represented the end of the town's Wild West lawlessness.

**50. Q:** What town was originally called "Cowford"?
**A:** Jacksonville. It had been named for a narrow spot on the St. Johns River where cattle could cross.

**51. Q:** How many times did President Andrew Jackson visit Jacksonville, which was named for him?
**A:** Never.

**52. Q:** What city was once called "Hogtown"?
**A:** Gainesville, home of the University of Florida and a center of pork production. It was later named for Seminole War Gen. Edmund Gaines, but "Hogtown" is still a nickname.

**53. Q:** What southern Palm Beach County town was originally named Linton and is now named for a neighborhood of Detroit?
**A:** Delray Beach. After a hard freeze, residents accused developer Col. William Linton of overstating the land's worth and renamed the town.

**54. Q:** What South Florida town is named for a lost continent?
**A:** Atlantis.

**55. Q:** What Florida town is named for a space vehicle?
**A:** Satellite Beach.

**56. Q:** How was Vero Beach named?
**A:** A woman from one of the pioneer families submitted the word, a variation on the Latin "veritas," or "truth."

**57. Q:** "Vaca" is Spanish for cow, but there are no cows on Vaca Key. How did it get its name?
**A:** Spaniards named it for the many nearby manatees, also known as sea cows.

Andrew Jackson
was Florida's first governor.

58. Q: Did Key West get its name because it is the westernmost of the Florida Keys as they curve under the Florida peninsula?
A: No. It is a bastardization of "Cayo Hueso," Spanish for "Island of Bones." That referred either to the bleached reefs and rocks of the island or to the animal bones scattered on the beach.

59. Q: For what is the southern Dade County town of Naranja named?
A: It's Spanish for "orange."

60. Q: Where did the Florida Keys island of Islamorada get its name?
A: "Islamorada" is Spanish for "purple island," a reference to the island's purple appearance from the ocean.

61. Q: Like New York, Florida has its own "Long Island." Where is it?
A: It's Key Largo — from Cayo Largo, Spanish for "long key." There's also a Long Key.

62. Q: What was the original name of the Panhandle town of Valparaiso?
A: Boggy. Valparaiso, by the way, is Spanish for "valley of paradise."

63. Q: What's the meaning behind the name of Interlachen, near Palatka?
A: The town is between two lakes; Interlachen is Scottish for "between lakes."

64. Q: What city's name reportedly comes from an Indian word for "sweet water"?
A: Miami.

65. Q: According to folklore, a group of surveyors visiting South Florida marked their map to remind themselves of an excellent fish they had there for dinner. The name stayed on the map. Name the Broward County town.
A: Pompano Beach.

66. Q: According to legend, how did Marathon get its name?
A: Weary workers on Henry Flagler's railroad to Key West used the term to complain about the long, laborious work being rushed to completion in the ailing Flagler's lifetime.

67. Q: According to legend, the Keys town of Tavernier was named for a billboard that advertised what?
A: "Tavern here."

68. Q: How was Cudjoe Key named?
A: Many believe it is a bastardization of "Cousin Joe," perhaps a one-time resident of the area.

69. Q: The town of O'Leno, in North Florida, was originally called "Kino." What is Kino?
A: A type of lottery game. Commercial and religious pressure prompted the name change. Bypass-ed by the railroad, the town dwindled and is now the site of a state park.

70. Q: How did Clearwater get its name?
A: Springs of fresh water bubbled along the shore, even under the waterline at low tide. With the effects of tides and changes made in the land by humans, the springs have all but disappeared.

71. Q: What major Florida city was almost named Detroit?
A: St. Petersburg. The two settlers drew straws, and Peter Demens, a native of St. Petersburg, Russia, won. Gen. John C. Williams, as a consolation prize, named the first commercial building—the Detroit Hotel—for his hometown.

72. Q: What's the source of the name for the town of Dania?
A: It was settled by families from Denmark.

73. **Q:** When settlers from Ossabaw, Ga., settled in Indian River County, how did they twist the name of their former hometown to name their new one?
    **A:** They turned it backwards and named the new town Wabasso.

74. **Q:** How did the town of Switz-erland, south of Jacksonville, get its name?
    **A:** It was founded by a Swiss native, Francis Philip Fatio Sr., who received 10,000 acres in 1763 from the British.

75. **Q:** What town is named for figures of Norse mythology?
    **A:** Valkaria. A Swede who helped found it named it for the Valkyries, maidens who selected who would die in battle and led the fallen to Valhalla, or heaven.

76. **Q:** What's the meaning behind the original name of Milton: Scratch Ankle?
    **A:** Because people landing boats there had to contend with briars that grew at the water's edge.

77. **Q:** How was Palm Beach County's Okeelanta farming area named?
    **A:** It lies between Lake Okeechobee and the Atlantic Ocean.

78. **Q:** What North Florida county seat is named for the historic home of the county's famous namesake?
    **A:** Jefferson County's seat, Monticello, is named for Thomas Jefferson's Virginia home.

79. **Q:** What city was originally Fort Dallas?
    **A:** Miami.

80. **Q:** What city was originally called Alligator?

**A:** Lake City.

81. **Q:** In 1918, a group of investors secretly buried a treasure chest filled with lead on the beach at a Pinellas County island, then dug it up and with great fanfare paraded it through the area. The ploy worked and the land sold. What's the name of the town that fol-lowed?
    **A:** Treasure Island.

82. **Q:** There's a Florida town named Venice, but what city claims to be "the Venice of America"?
    **A:** Fort Lauderdale, with its 270 miles of inland waterways, makes that claim. The Florida town named for the Italian city is near Sarasota.

83. **Q:** What town's nickname is "The Magic City"?
    **A:** Miami.

84. **Q:** What Florida city has been dubbed "The City of The Future"?
    **A:** Miami.

85. **Q:** What's the name of the town midway between Tallahassee and Quincy in the Panhandle?
    **A:** Midway.

86. **Q:** Where will you find Paradise?
    **A:** The tiny settlement is just north of Gainesville.

87. **Q:** What two towns are right next to Paradise?
    **A:** Adam and Eve.

88. **Q:** What two Florida towns share the nickname "The City Beautiful"?
    **A:** Coral Gables and Orlando.

89. **Q:** What area calls itself "Florida's First Coast"?

A: Jacksonville and its beaches.

90. Q: By what name are the ocean-front areas of Dade, Broward, and Palm Beach counties collectively known?
A: "The Gold Coast."

91. Q: Why is the area encompassing Martin, St. Lucie, and Indian River counties called the Treasure Coast?
A: Because many shipwrecks lie offshore.

92. Q: Brevard County got what nick-name from the modernistic industry that put it on the map?
A: "The Space Coast" honors the area's space exploration industry, centered at the Kennedy Space Center at Cape Canaveral.

93. Q: What part of Florida is nick-named "The Emerald Coast"?
A: The beaches of the Panhandle, for their clear, green gulf waters.

94. Q: What part of Florida is called "The Miracle Strip"?
A: The beach resort areas around Panama City.

95. Q: What area of Florida is some-times derisively called the "Redneck Riviera"?
A: Florida's Panhandle, the beach playground for Southerners.

96. Q: How did Coconut Grove's Dinner Key get its name?
A: It was a popular early 20th-century picnic site.

97. Q: How did southwest Florida's Corkscrew Swamp get its name?

A: A crooked creek winds and twists through the swamp.

98. Q: What central Florida river was originally called "Rio de la Paz"?
A: It's now known by the English translation: Peace River.

99. Q: What's the meaning behind the name of the Tamiami Trail?
A: The road goes from Tampa to Miami.

100. Q: What did the romantic beach road known as A1A used to be called?
A: State Road 1. People kept con-fusing it with nearby U.S. 1, so the state changed the name in 1946.

101. Q: What city has a "Miracle Mile"?
A: Coral Gables.

102. Q: What was the original name of Florida's Turnpike?
A: The Sunshine State Parkway.

103. Q: In 1890, businessmen devel-oped a 7-1/2 mile railroad linking Jupiter with Juno Beach. They named two other stops Mars and Venus. What did they cleverly dub the operation?
A: "The Celestial Railroad." It lasted only six years.

104. Q: What's the former name of the University of Central Florida in Orlando?
A: Florida Technological University, or Florida Tech.

# 4

# *Let's Go to the Map*

1. **Q:** Why is it that in Florida, as the expression goes, "the further north you go the further south you get"?
**A:** Because South Florida, with its many Yankee transplants, is more like the northern United States and much of North Florida remains part of the old South.

2. **Q:** How much of Florida is more than 60 miles from the nearest salt water?
**A:** None of it.

3. **Q:** What's further east, Tallahassee or Pittsburgh, Pa.?
**A:** Pittsburgh. Because of the North American coastline's jog to the east, most of Florida is west of the northeastern United States. Jacksonville is directly south of Cleveland, Ohio, and 837 miles west of a line extending south from Maine's northeastern shore. Pensacola is directly south of Chicago.

4. **Q:** How much of Florida is south of California's southern border?
**A:** Florida's northernmost point is 100 miles south of California's southernmost point and 1,700 miles from the equator, closer than any other state in the continental United States.

5. **Q:** What fraction of South America is directly south of Miami?
**A:** None of it. The entire continent lies east of Florida.

6. **Q:** The distance from the Georgia line to Florida's southern tip, at Key West, is as far as the distance from Boston to what major eastern seaboard city?
**A:** The 447-mile stretch is as far as Boston is from Washington, D.C.

7. **Q:** The length of the Panhandle equals the distance from Norfolk, Va., to what major northeastern city?
**A:** From the northeast corner, at Fort Clinch, to the western end, at Pensacola, is 361 miles - the distance from Norfolk to New York City.

8. **Q:** The distance from Key West to Pensacola exceeds the distance from Albany, N.Y., to what major Midwestern city?
**A:** The 805 miles is farther than the distance from Albany to Chicago.

9. **Q:** Florida's peninsular coastline is as long as Kansas City is far from what major northeastern city?

23

A: The coastline, wrapping around from Fernandina Beach to the Keys, up to the Panhandle, and west to Pensacola, stretches about 1,300 miles—the distance from Kansas City to New York.

10. Q: If you made Florida's snaking coastline of inlets and bays a straight line, it would stretch from Washington, D.C., to what foreign capital?
A: Manila, Philippines. Florida's 8,400-mile coastline is the nation's second longest, behind Alaska.

11. Q: What fraction of the trip from Miami to Dallas, Texas, is in Florida?
A: Half.

12. Q: What fraction of the trip from Miami to Los Angeles is in Florida?
A: One fourth.

13. Q: What fraction of the trip from Miami to New York is in Florida?
A: One fourth.

14. Q: Tallahassee is farther from Miami than from the capitals of how many other states?
A: Five. Florida's capital is 468 miles from the state's most important city—farther than from the capitals of Alabama, Georgia, South Carolina, Mississippi, and Louisiana.

15. Q: What major American highway begins—or ends—in front of the Monroe County Courthouse in Key West?
A: U.S. 1. It snakes 2,467 miles up the Atlantic coast to Fort Kent, Maine.

16. Q: What are the numbered green signs on U.S. 1 in the Keys used for?

A: They're mile markers, showing the distance from Key West, and are the most common form of address in the Keys.

17. Q: How long is the famous Seven Mile Bridge in the Florida Keys?
A: It's not quite seven miles, but 35,716 feet—6.76 miles.

18. Q: What stretches 309 miles from Wildwood to Homestead?
A: Florida's Turnpike.

19. Q: The first leg of the Sunshine State Parkway—now Florida's Turnpike—went from Fort Pierce to what city?
A: Miami.

20. Q: What can you find every mile on Florida's Turnpike?
A: Motorist Aid telephone call boxes.

21. Q: Interstate 95, which starts in Maine, ends in the downtown area of what Florida city?
A: Miami. The interstate passes through 16 states, more than any other.

22. Q: What two Florida cities form the ends of Interstate 4?
A: Daytona Beach and Tampa.

23. Q: Why does Interstate 4 have the interstate highway system's smallest assigned number?
A: The expressways are numbered on a giant grid, radiating from the southwestern United States. North-south expressways have odd numbers, east-west expressways even numbers, and I-4 is the southernmost east-west route.

24. Q: Interstate 10, which crosses the continent from Santa Monica, Calif., ends at what Florida city?
A: Jacksonville.

**25. Q:** A historic trail marking what explorer's march runs from the Tampa area to north of Tallahassee and will eventually stretch to Arkansas?
**A:** The De Soto Trail, which marks Hernando de Soto's expedition, the first by Europeans into the interior of North America.

The De Soto Trail runs from Tampa to near Tallahassee. (State of Florida)

**26. Q:** What historic trail extends from St. Augustine to Jacksonville and west to the Alabama state line near Pensacola?
**A:** The Old Spanish Trail, which connected dozens of Spanish missions across colonial Florida and on to San Diego, Calif.

**27. Q:** The "Black Bear Trail" went from Montréal to what Florida city?
**A:** St. Petersburg.

**28. Q:** What route is retraced by the Florida Cracker Trail, a 150-mile long, official state trail stretching across the peninsula from Bradenton to Fort Pierce?
**A:** It retraces the route 19th-century cowboys used to drive cattle to market.

**29. Q:** What's the name of the protected water route that follows the eastern seaboard from Miami to New Jersey?
**A:** The Intracoastal Waterway, a connected system of inland channels for commercial and pleasure boat traffic, extends 1,391 miles up the Atlantic coast.

**30. Q:** What's the only inland waterway across the peninsula?
**A:** The Okeechobee Waterway—from the St. Lucie River to Lake Okeechobee and west down the Caloosahatchee River—connects Stuart to Fort Myers.

**31. Q:** What must you do when you cross the Apalachicola River in North Florida?
**A:** Change your clock; all of the Panhandle west of the river is in the Central Time Zone.

**32. Q:** How many counties does Florida have?
**A:** Sixty-seven.

**33. Q:** How many of Florida's 67 counties border another state?
**A:** Only 14. The rest border only each other or the ocean.

**34. Q:** Since 1821, two-thirds of Florida's 67 counties have been cut from which single county?
**A:** The original St. Johns County, established in 1821 by territorial governor Andrew Jackson, once encompassed all of Florida east of the Suwannee River and spanned 1,100 miles of coastline. It has since been reduced in size from 39,400 square miles to 609.

**35. Q:** Which major Florida city was originally in Mosquito County?
**A:** Orlando, now in Orange County.

36. **Q:** Whatever happened to Fayette County?
**A:** Florida's lost county was formed in 1832 along the Apalachicola River in the Panhandle and named for French hero Marquis de Lafayette, who helped the Americans in the Revolutionary War. It was later swallowed by adjacent Jackson County.

37. **Q:** How much of Duval County is taken up by the city of Jacksonville?
**A:** All of it. In 1968, city fathers consolidated services by expanding city limits to county lines. That made Jacksonville, in size, one of the largest cities in America. It's 840 square miles, bigger than the giant Lake Okeechobee.

Jacksonville and Duval County merged in 1968. (City of Jacksonville)

38. **Q:** Daytona Beach is not the Volusia county seat. What town is?
**A:** DeLand.

39. **Q:** Was Mobile, Ala., ever part of Florida?
**A:** It was part of the territory of West Florida, which stretched almost to New Orleans before it was shrunk and combined with East Florida to form the present borders.

40. **Q:** According to the 2000 census, where is Florida's center of population—the point at which an equal number of people live north, south, east, and west?
**A:** It's in an orange grove in southern Polk County. That county has hosted the center since the 1960s.

41. **Q:** Where will you find the Palm Beach County towns of Bean City, Chosen, and Okeelanta?
**A:** You won't. The farm towns near Lake Okeechobee were dev-

A causeway between Miami and Miami Beach is named for World War II hero Douglas MacArthur. (Time Life Television)

astated by the 1928 hurricane and faded away.

42. What World War II general has a causeway from Miami to Miami Beach named for him?
**A:** Douglas MacArthur.

43. **Q:** The tiny Polk County community of Nalcrest was built exclusively for retired workers of what profession?
**A:** Postal workers.

44. **Q:** What south-central Florida town did Henry Flagler brag would be the "Chicago of Florida" when he established it?
**A:** Okeechobee. The town is now more famous for bass fishing and mobile homes.

# 5
# *B u s i n e s s   a n d   T o u r i s m*

1. **Q:** What nickname has been given to the northerners who flock to Florida every winter?
   **A:** Snowbirds.

2. **Q:** In the 1800s, Florida's snowbird capital wasn't Miami, but rather what city?
   **A:** Jacksonville.

3. **Q:** What's the top state of origin for air travelers to Florida?
   **A:** New York.

4. **Q:** What's the top state of origin for motor tourists visiting Florida?
   **A:** Georgia.

5. **Q:** In the 1964 film *Where the Boys Are*, where are the boys?
   **A:** In Fort Lauderdale, the college spring break capital.

6. **Q:** What city proclaims its oceanfront "The World's Most Famous Beach"?
   **A:** Daytona Beach.

7. **Q:** Where can you park your car in Daytona Beach?
   **A:** Right on the beach.

8. **Q:** People gather every day at Key West's Mallory Pier to view what atmospheric phenomenon?
   **A:** They gather to see—and applaud—what's been called the world's most beautiful sunset.

9. **Q:** What do people like to collect on the beach at Sanibel Island?
   **A:** Shells. Its shallow offshore waters and a strong inbound current dump untold numbers of shells on the beach. People armed with plastic bags can be seen year-round doing the "Sanibel stoop" — bending over the sand to pick up shells.

10. **Q:** What foreign language are you likely to hear in Hollywood?
    **A:** French. It is a haven for snowbirds from Quebec.

11. **Q:** What's unusual about the design of the Venetian Pool in Coral Gables?
    **A:** The pool is a natural swimming hole; a spring-fed lagoon decorated with caves, waterfalls, and arched bridges.

27

## I'M GOING TO...

12. **Q:** What's the world's top tourist destination?
    **A:** Walt Disney World. Its four parks reportedly draw 40 million visitors a year.

13. **Q:** What's the world's biggest amusement resort?
    **A:** Again, Walt Disney World. Its 30,000 acres straddle Orange and Osceola counties.

14. **Q:** What's bigger, Walt Disney World or New York's Manhattan Island?
    **Q:** The Central Florida attraction, opened in 1971, sprawls over about 47 square miles, making it twice the size of Manhattan.

15. **Q:** What does EPCOT, at Walt Disney World, stand for?
    **A:** Experimental Prototype Community of Tomorrow.

16. **Q:** What's the name of the 180-foot-high sphere at the center of Walt Disney World's EPCOT?
    **A:** Spaceship Earth.

17. **Q:** For what has one-third of Walt Disney World's property been set aside?
    **A:** A wilderness preserve.

18. **Q:** What will you find under the Magic Kingdom at Walt Disney World?
    **A:** One and a half miles of tunnels for "cast members" to get around under the attraction.

19. **Q:** In an average year, Walt Disney World sells enough of what to circle the world three times?

Walt Disney World is the world's top tourist destination. (Walt Disney Company)

    **A:** French Fries: 9 million pounds of them. It also serves 10 million hot dogs, 7 million hamburgers and 50 million soft drinks.

20. **Q:** What's Osceola County's biggest city during the day?
    **A:** Walt Disney World. With 54,000 cast members, including some 650 horticulture specialists and 4,000 entertainers, it's bigger than the county seat of Kissimmee, population about 48,000. And that doesn't even count the visitors.

21. **Q:** What major industry set up shop in the late 1980s in central Florida, with not one but two sprawling facilities?
    **A:** Film-making got going in Florida in a big way with the opening of the Disney-MGM studios and Universal studios, both near Orlando.

22. **Q:** How is Orlando ranked among American cities in total hotel rooms?
**A:** It's second, with more than 114,000, and gaining on Las Vegas, which has about 126,000.

23. **Q:** What feature at Orlando's Hyatt Regency Grand Cypress is one of the largest in the world?
**A:** An 800,000-gallon pool.

24. **Q:** What unusual guests spend their days in the lobby of Orlando's Peabody Hotel?
**A:** Every day, the hotel rolls out a red carpet for five mallard ducks that emerge from an elevator amid a rousing march tune and waddle to an ornate marble fountain, where they spend the day.

25. **Q:** What's unusual about a lodge near Key Largo?
**A:** It's under water. Jules' Undersea Lodge claims to be the only hotel in the world that's completely under water. Guests must dive to it.

26. **Q:** What Central Florida body of water hosts the state's oldest commercial tourist attraction?
**Q:** Silver Springs. The glass bottom boat attraction opened in the 1890s.

27. **Q:** How did Silver Springs get its name?
**A:** Tiny shards of limestone and shell swirl in its waters, sparkling in the sun.

Silver Springs, around 1886 (State Photographic Archives)

28. **Q:** Green Cove Springs, southwest of Jacksonville, was a fashionable resort in the 1870s and 1880s. What did hucksters claim its 3,000-gallon-a-minute spring to be?
**A:** The Fountain of Youth.

29. **Q:** What is the favorite way to get downstream at Ichetucknee Springs State Park north of Gainesville?
**A:** In inner tubes. As many as 3,000 people a day take the leisurely ride down the clear stream at about a mile an hour. Even in the heat of summer, the temperature is constantly a chilly 73 degrees.

You can't valet park at Jules' Undersea Lodge. (Jules' Undersea Lodge)

30. **Q:** The Monument of the States tourist attraction in Kissimmee is a pyramid containing 1,500 of what item?
**A:** Stones, from 48 American states and some two dozen foreign countries.

31. **Q:** What sea-oriented attraction is near St. Augustine?
**A:** Marineland of Florida.

32. **Q:** What attraction in Dade City, east of Tampa, honors Florida's early settlers?
**A:** The Florida Pioneer Museum.

33. **Q:** A model of the ship in what famous movie of the same name was docked in St. Petersburg and Miami?
**A:** The Bounty, as in *Mutiny on the Bounty.* The tourist attraction had been in St. Petersburg, then moved to Miami's Bayside shopping and tourism area. It moved to New England in the early 1990s.

The *Bounty* was a waterfront attraction in St. Petersburg and Miami. (*Bounty* Exhibit)

34. **Q:** What happens every half hour at the Bok Tower in Lake Wales?
**A:** The tower's 53 bells, ranging in weight from 17 pounds to nearly 12 tons, chime across the surrounding countryside. The tower and its adjoining 128-acre natural gardens were built by Dutch-born publisher and Pulitzer Prize-winning author Edward Bok in 1929 in gratitude to his adopted land.

35. **Q:** A museum in Kissimmee honors what rock and roll legend?
**A:** Elvis Presley. The museum has about 300 items that once belonged to "The King."

36. **Q:** Where's America's fourth-largest Navy base?
**A:** Mayport Naval Station, near Jacksonville.

37. **Q:** What's the ritzy street on Palm Beach whose shops are said to rival those of Beverly Hills' Rodeo Drive and New York City's Fifth Avenue for chic?
**A:** Worth Avenue.

38. **Q:** By what name is the former Deering estate near downtown Miami better known?
**A:** Vizcaya. The house is now a museum.

39. **Q:** Where is the Florida State Fair?
**A:** Tampa. Unlike other states, Florida is dominated by regional fairs that draw far more than the official state event.

40. **Q:** Florida Southern College in Lakeland has the largest collection on one site of buildings designed by what famous architect?
**A:** Frank Lloyd Wright. His design is the only existing example of his planning concept called "organic architecture," in which cities are decentralized. He planned 18 buildings, of which seven were completed between 1938 and 1959.

41. Q: Where's the winter headquarters of the Ringling Brothers & Barnum and Bailey Circus?
A: It moved its winter home from Connecticut to Sarasota in 1927, to Venice in 1960, and to the Florida State Fairgrounds in Tampa in 1993.

42. Q: What's Florida's biggest art festival?
A: The Coconut Grove Art Festival, which celebrated its 40th anniversary in 2003.

43. Q: What ethnic group celebrates the Goombay Festival in Coconut Grove?
A: The festival in Miami's eclectic enclave celebrates the area's Bahamian heritage.

44. Q: What event does the "King Mango Strut" in Miami's Coconut Grove spoof?
A: The King Orange Jamboree parade. The Mango Strut outlived the larger parade, which had its last run in 2001, ending after 65 years.

45. Q: What's the most popular mode of transportation for tourists coming to Florida?
A: In 1988, for the first time, more tourists flew than drove to Florida.

46. What's Florida's busiest airport?
A: Miami International.

47. Q: How much did traffic increase at Orlando International Airport in the 1980s?
A: It more than doubled. By 2004, it was the 16th busiest in the United States and 28th busiest in the world with about 700 commercial operations a day.

48. Q: Which Miami-based airline did World War I ace Eddie Rickenbacker take over in 1935 and take from obscurity to world prominence?
A: The now-defunct Eastern.

49. Q: Whatever happened to Mackey Airlines, which flew between several Florida cities and the Bahamas in the 1950s?
A: The carrier, which began in 1953, merged eight years later with Eastern; by then it was carrying 150,000 passengers a year.

50. Q: How does Miami's cruise ship port rank in the world?
A: It's the world's top port, serving 3.6 million passengers a year.

51. Q: What do the abbreviations MIA, FLL and PBI on your luggage tags mean?
A: They are the official three-letter designations for the Miami, Fort Lauderdale-Hollywood and Palm Beach international airports.

52. Q: Why is Orlando International Airport's 3-letter designation MCO?
A: It was once the McCoy Air Force Base.

53. Q: The Auto Train, which ferries both passengers and their cars, starts in Lorton, Va., near Washington D.C., and ends in what central Florida town?
A: Sanford, north of Orlando.

54. Q: What sports industry around Ocala injects about $2.2 billion into the state?
A: The breeding of race horses. About 85 percent of the state's thoroughbred farms are in Marion County.

55. Q: How does Florida rank in earnings in top stakes thoroughbred horse races?
A: It's second only to Kentucky.

56. **Q:** The Ron Jon shop in Cocoa Beach claims to be the largest of its kind in the world. What does it sell?
**A:** Surfing equipment.

57. **Q:** What businesses do the Keys have more of per mile than any other place in the world?
**A:** Dive shops.

58. **Q:** In 1988, Florida governor Bob Martinez proposed the government and the private sector build America's first commercial port for what mode of travel?
**A:** It would be the country's first commercial spaceport. The facility, based at Cape San Blas in the Panhandle, launched its first rocket from a mobile launcher in Mexico 1991 and its second from Cape San Blas on August 22, 1993.

59. **Q:** The international headquarters for what hamburger chain are in Miami-Dade county?

**A:** Burger King.

60. **Q:** How much did greater Orlando's population increase from 1970 to the mid-1980s?
**A:** It more than doubled. By 2004, more than 1.8 million people lived in Orange, Osceola, Seminole and Lake counties.

61. **Q:** What fraction of Florida's new businesses set up shop in Orlando in the first half of the 1980s?
**A:** Half.

62. **Q:** What Florida town had the nation's highest per capita income in the mid-1800s?
**A:** Key West, thanks mostly to the lucrative trade in salvaging shipwrecks.

63. **Q:** How does agriculture rank among Florida industries?
**A:** The $62 billion industry is second only to tourism.

## COME TO THE FLORIDA SUNSHINE TREE

64. **Q:** What fraction of America's citrus is grown in Florida?
**A:** About 80 percent of the grapefruit and oranges. Florida also supplies 90 percent of the American demand for orange juice.

65. **Q:** What happens to 95 percent of the oranges grown in Florida?
**A:** They're squeezed for orange juice concentrate. The same goes for about two thirds of the grapefruit. Orange juice accounts for about 61 percent of the pure juice consumed in America.

66. **Q:** Besides eating and juicing, what else can you make with oranges?

**A:** Wine, slushes, marmalades, syrup, alcohol, candies, jellies, perfume, soap, cosmetics, pharmaceuticals, paints, insecticides, rubber, textiles, ice cream, and cattle feed.

67. **Q:** What fruit crop did a close friend of French emperor Napoleon Bonaparte introduce to Florida in 1823?
**A:** Grapefruit.

Rows of orange trees fill the Central Florida countryside. (*Miami News*)

**68. Q:** What tasty fruit is the subject of a festival every year in Plant City, near Tampa?
**A:** Strawberries.

**69. Q:** What sweet crop now prevalent in South Florida was once big in North Florida?
**A:** Sugar. Indian raids during the Second Seminole War destroyed the industry in a matter of weeks and it never recovered.

**70. Q:** How does Florida rank nationally in production of sugar?
**A:** First.

**71. Q:** What fraction of America's sugar is grown in Florida?
**A:** About one-quarter.

**72. Q:** What fraction of the world's sugar crop comes from Florida?
**A:** About 1-1/2 percent.

**73. Q:** What fraction of the state's sugar crop comes from South Florida?
**A:** Virtually all of it.

**74. Q:** What two regions of Florida both claim to be America's "winter vegetable basket"?
**A:** The Everglades Agricultural Area, south of Lake Okeechobee, and the Homestead-South Dade area.

**75. Q:** Southwest Florida's Hardee County once bragged about being the world's capital for what green vegetable?
**A:** Cucumbers.

**76. Q:** Taylor County, southeast of Tallahassee, claims to be the top producing county in the South of what product?
**A:** Timber.

**77. Q:** The small island of Cedar Key,

Workers assemble millions of cigars a day. (Tampa News Bureau)

on the northern Gulf Coast, was a major timber town in the late 19th century. What was one of its key products?
**A:** Pencils.

**78. Q:** At its height, workers in Tampa's Ybor City made one million per day of what aromatic item?
**A:** Cigars. The industry is a fraction of its former size, and much of Ybor City is now a tourist destination.

**79. Q:** What did "El Lector" do as workers assembled cigars in Tampa and Key West?
**A:** He read them the day's newspaper or a book.

**80. Q:** In August, the quiet countryside around Live Oak, in the Panhandle, rings with the calls of auctioneers. What are they selling?
**A:** Tobacco.

**81. Q:** Florida is the third biggest state east of the Mississippi in what animal enterprise?
**A:** Cattle. There are some two million cows, 985,000 of them beef cows.

82. **Q:** What is more commercially caught off Florida's coast, shellfish or fish?
**A:** According to 2001 figures, fishermen harvested more fish but the shellfish was worth more. They caught about 57 million pounds of fish, worth about $69 million "off the boat" and about three to four times that at the seafood counter. They pulled up only 45 million pounds of shrimp, shellfish, clams, and other non-fish seafood, but its "off the boat" value was about $109 million. Overfishing and tougher regulations have dropped the totals; in 1995, they were 112 million pounds for fish and 52 million for shellfish.

83. **Q:** Does Florida import more fish and seafood than it produces?
**A:** Yes. In 2003, the state imported 4 billion pounds, worth $11 billion.

84. **Q:** For what ocean product is Tarpon Springs, north of St. Petersburg, famous?
**A:** Sponges. The mostly Greek town was "The Sponge Capital of the World" until the 1940s and 1950s, when the industry was reduced by a 1947 marine blight, development of synthetic sponges and resumption of the trade in postwar Europe.

85. **Q:** In its heyday, what fraction of America's oysters was harvested in Apalachicola Bay?
**A:** One-seventh. Overfishing, pollution, and increasing salinity have diminished oyster beds. The figure is now about 10 percent.

## FLORIDA'S MINES

86. **Q:** What fertilizer product is heavily mined in Florida?
**A:** Phosphate.

87. **Q:** What fraction of America's fertilizer phosphate is mined in Central Florida?
**A:** Seventy-five percent.

88. **Q:** What fraction of the world's fertilizer phosphate is mined in Central Florida?
**A:** One-fifth.

89. **Q:** What product used in painting was once distilled in large volume in North and Central Florida?
**A:** Turpentine. The advent of giant distilleries in the World War II era eventually put the smaller operations out of business.

# 6
# *Sports*

1.  **Q:** What military leader who chased Seminoles in the Everglades in 1857 would later gain fame for creating a sport with a big Florida connection?
    **A:** Gen. Abner Doubleday was at one time credited with inventing baseball, although historians now discount that. The game was first played in the 1840s and 1850s and grew to national prominence. At the end of the 19th century, Florida emerged as a center for spring training.

2.  **Q:** What's the nickname of Florida's spring training operations for major league baseball teams?
    **A:** The Grapefruit League.

3.  **Q:** What town hosted the first baseball spring training?
    **A:** Jacksonville hosted the Washington Statesmen of the National League in 1888. The practice had begun two years earlier when the Philadelphia Phillies trained at Charleston, S.C., and the Chicago White Stockings—later the White Sox—at Hot Springs, Ark.

4.  **Q:** According to a 1913 newspaper article, the playing of what sport on Sunday was forbidden in Panama City "by the laws of Florida and the law of God?"
    **A:** Baseball.

5.  **Q:** Tinker Field baseball stadium in Orlando is named for one-third of what great combination?
    **A:** Joe Tinker, president and general manager of the Orlando Florida State League team in the 1920s and later a real-estate speculator, was the Tinker of "Tinker to Evers to Chance," the Chicago Cubs' great double-play combination.

6.  **Q:** What baseball legend reportedly hit a record-breaking home run in Tampa in 1919?
    **A:** Babe Ruth. The shot, the longest for a preseason game at the time, went 587 feet.

7.  **Q:** What baseball star, while vacationing in Florida in 1930, threatened to retire and play golf unless he was paid more to hit home runs?
    **A:** Babe Ruth. Relaxing in Palm Beach, he demanded what was then an outrageous sum: $85,000. He rejected a $75,000 offer.

8.  **Q:** What famous baseball player was ordered by Sanford's police chief to leave a spring training game?
    **A:** The Brooklyn Dodgers' Jackie Robinson, who on April 11, 1947, became the first black to play major league baseball. The state yanked the welcome mat for Robinson. Daytona Beach officials reminded the Dodgers he would have to stay in a segregated hotel. Jacksonville officials canceled a game rather than have him play. Sanford officials said blacks and whites could not play on the same field, so Robinson returned to Daytona Beach. At a later game in Sanford, he batted in the first inning but he and a black teammate were ordered to leave the field in the second inning. The minor league field in Daytona Beach is now named for Jackie Robinson.

9.  **Q:** In 1982, 1985, 1999, and 2001 the University of Miami returned from Omaha, Neb., with national championships in what sport?
    **A:** Baseball.

10. **Q:** When the city of St. Petersburg built a domed professional baseball stadium in 1989, what major component did it lack?
    **A:** A team. The town suffered no less than seven failed attempts at a major league team between 1984 and 1992. It finally got the new Tampa Bay Devil Rays franchise in 1995 and the team began play in 1998.

11. **Q:** What major league baseball team came ever so close to moving to St. Petersburg's new dome in 1988?
    **A:** The Chicago White Sox. It took an 11th-hour bill by the state legislature to fund a new stadium to keep the team in Illinois. The others: Minnesota Twins (1984), Oakland Athletics (1985), Texas Rangers (1988), expansion team (1991), Seattle Mariners (1992), and San Francisco Giants (1992).

12. **Q:** Florida hosts a school for what sports occupation?
    **A:** Umpiring. The camp for baseball's most unpopular job is in Ormond Beach.

13. **Q:** What famous baseball announcer retired to Tallahassee?
    **A:** Red Barber, who did Brooklyn Dodgers, New York Yankees, World Series games and sports commentaries for a half century. He died at 84 on October 22, 1992.

Red Barber was a baseball broadcasting legend for a half century.

14. **Q:** What legendary red-headed football star retired to the small Osceola county town of Indian Lake Estates?
    **A:** Red Grange. He died in January, 1991, at 86.

Red Grange was "the Galloping Ghost."

15. **Q:** What's Florida's largest major football stadium?
    **A:** Ben Hill Griffin Stadium at Florida Field in Gainesville can hold 88,548. Runners-up are Florida State's Doak Campbell Stadium (82,300), Jacksonville's Alltell Stadium (82,000), and Miami's Pro Player Stadium (75,540).

16. **Q:** What are the college team names for Miami, Florida, and Florida State?
    **A:** The Hurricanes, the Gators, and the Seminoles.

## PRIDE OF THE GATORS

17. **Q:** What players from Florida colleges have won the prestigious Heisman Trophy, awarded to the nation's best college football player?
    **A:** UF's Steve Spurrier—who would be named that school's head football coach in 1989—won it in 1966. University of Miami quarterback Vinny Testaverde won exactly 20 years later, in 1986. Fellow Hurricane Gino Torretta won it in 1992. The next year, quarterback Charlie Ward became the first winner from Florida State. Gator Danny Wuerffel, coached by Spurrier, won in 1996, and Chris Weinke of Florida State won in 2000.

18. **Q:** What does the announcer holler when the UF football team takes the field?
    **A:** H-e-e-e-r-e come the Gators!

19. **Q:** At most UF home football games since 1949, Tampa insurance agent George Edmondson goes from section to section, appearing suddenly from a tunnel and leading the crowd in a certain cheer. What's his nickname?
    **A:** Mr. Two-Bits.

20. **Q:** At the end of the third quarter of every UF football game, fans place hands on each others' shoulders around the stadium and sway to what traditional song?
    **A:** "We are the Boys of Old Florida."

21. **Q:** In the 1920s and 1930s, UF freshmen had to wear orange and blue beanies called "rat caps" until Christmas vacation—unless what happened?
    **A:** Unless the Gators beat the University of Georgia in football in the fall.

22. **Q:** What annual sporting event at Alltell Stadium has been dubbed "the world's largest outdoor cocktail party"?
    **A:** The football game between the Gators and the Georgia Bulldogs.

23. **Q:** What's the name of the pep rally and night of skits that highlights UF's football homecoming weekend?
    **A:** Gator Growl.

24. **Q:** What national sports drink was invented at UF?
    **A:** Gatorade.

25. **Q:** What did the UF football team do November 18, 1984, that the school had been unable to do in 51 years?
    **A:** They won a championship in the NCAA's Southeastern Conference, ending a drought that had obsessed Gator fans. Three days later, the Gators were stripped of the crown. They had been placed on probation earlier in the year for 107 NCAA violations. The Gators won their first legitimate SEC title in 1991 and others in 1993, 1994, 1995, 1996, and 2000.

## HURRICANE WARNINGS

26. Q: Which of Florida's three major colleges plays its football games off campus?
A: The University of Miami plays at the Orange Bowl.

27. Q: What did the University of Miami do on January 3, 1984, that no other Florida college had done?
A: They brought a national college football championship to Florida. Just after midnight, with 48 seconds left in the 50th Orange Bowl game, they stopped the top-ranked Nebraska Cornhuskers on a two-point play, preserving a 31-30 win.

The University of Miami brought the state its first national football championship in 1983-1984. (*Miami News*)

28. Q: When the University of Miami became the state's first-ever national college football champion during the 1983-1984 season, it had not gone undefeated. Who beat the Hurricanes that year?
A: Their cross-state rivals, the Florida Gators, beat the Hurricanes 28-3 in Miami's opener. Miami didn't lose again that season.

29. Q: How many football national championships have been won by Florida colleges?

A: Eight. The University of Miami won in the 1983, 1987, 1989, 1991, and 2001 seasons; Florida State won in 1993 and 1999 and Florida in 1996.

30. Q: What special effect do cheerleaders generate when the University of Miami Hurricanes run onto the football field?
A: They set off smoke machines, simulating the winds of a storm.

31. Q: What animal roams the sidelines at football games as the University of Miami Hurricanes mascot?
A: A giant bird called an ibis. According to legend, the ibis is the first bird to return after a hurricane.

32. Q: What does a horseman do on the 50-yard-line at the start of every Florida State University football game?
A: The colorful rider, dressed in Seminole garb, stabs a giant flaming spear into the ground to fire up fans.

33. Q: What Florida college discontinued its football program in 1975?
A: Tampa University.

34. Q: What was unusual about Pat Palinkas' appearance in a minor league football game in Orlando on August 15, 1970?
A: Pat's a she—the first woman to play in a professional football game

# THE MIAMI DOLPHINS

35. **Q:** What comedian was an early part-owner of the Miami Dolphins football team?
    **A:** Danny Thomas.

36. **Q:** What did the Miami Dolphins do on January 14, 1973, that no NFL football team had ever done before or since?
    **A:** They won the 1973 Super Bowl and finished 17-0; an undefeated "perfect season."

37. **Q:** What two South Florida expressways are named for a local professional sports team and its coach, respectively?

**A:** The Dolphin Expressway—State Road 836—and the Don Shula Expressway—State Road 874—both in Dade County.

38. **Q:** What did Miami Dolphin greats Larry Csonka, Jim Kiick and Paul Warfield do in 1974 that set the National Football League on its ear?
    **A:** They jumped to the fledgling World Football League in a package for the then-outrageous figure of $3 million. Despite the acquisition of the three and other big names, the league only lasted a season and a half.

39. **Q:** What professional sports entity came into being in Florida on April 24, 1974?
    **A:** The Tampa Bay Buccaneers football team.

40. **Q:** What was unusual about the Tampa Bay Buccaneers NFL football team's first season in 1976?
    **A:** They failed to win any of their 14 games.

Miami's Orange Bowl has hosted five Super Bowls, including Super Bowl II.
(*Miami News*)

41. **Q:** Through 2004, how does Florida rank for hosting Super Bowls?
    **A:** Florida and California are tied for first with 11. New Orleans alone has hosted nine. Florida Super Bowls: 1967, 1968, 1970, 1976, and 1979 in Miami's Orange Bowl; 1989, 1995 and 1999 in Joe Robbie (now Pro Player) Stadium north of Miami; and 1984, 1991 and 2001 in Tampa Stadium, now Raymond James Stadium.

Joe Namath guaranteed it, and the upstart American Football League took Super Bowl III. (*Miami News*)

United States Football League?
**A:** Burt Reynolds; the team was named for his character in the *Smokey and the Bandit* film series.

46. **Q:** What Miami Dolphins legend was general manager of the United States Football League's Jacksonville Bulls?
**A:** Larry Csonka.

47. **Q:** What modern game did early natives on the Pinellas peninsula approximate?
**A:** Basketball. The Indians' crude game involved throwing a round gourd at a piece of thatch atop a pole.

48. **Q:** What Florida colleges did UCLA beat in 1970 and 1972, respectively, in the NCAA college basketball championship?
**A:** UCLA beat Jacksonville University in 1970 and Florida State in 1972. The California school won 10 of 12 championships between 1964 and 1975. In 1994, Florida became the only other state school to reach the Final Four, but the Gators lost in the semifinal game.

49. **Q:** What are Florida's two National Basketball Association teams?
**A:** The Miami Heat and the Orlando Magic.

50. **Q:** What's responsible for more than 2,800 holes in Palm Beach County?
**A:** It had 119 golf courses as of 2003, the most of any county in Florida.

51. **Q:** Where did Florida rank nationally in number of golf courses as of 2003?
**A:** First, with 1,081 of the 15,902 monitored by the National Golf

42. **Q:** On January 12, 1969, at Miami's Orange Bowl, three days after saying "I'll guarantee it," an athlete did what he had promised and forever changed the face of his sport. What did he do?
**A:** New York Jets quarterback "Broadway Joe" Namath led his team to a 16-7 win over the Baltimore Colts—the prohibitive favorite—in Super Bowl III. The win, first ever for the American Football League, gave the league instant credibility, even as it prepared to merge with the National Football League.

43. **Q:** The championship of what professional football league was played in Tampa in 1984?
**A:** The United States Football League.

44. **Q:** What Florida cities had teams in the 1980s' short-lived United States Football league?
**A:** Three: the Orlando Renegades, Jacksonville Bulls and Tampa Bay Bandits.

45. **Q:** What well-known Florida actor was a part-owner of the Tampa Bay Bandits of the now-defunct

Foundation. That's one out of every 13-1/2 courses in the United States.

52. **Q:** How many of America's top ten metropolitan areas in population per hole of golf were in Florida as of 1993?
    **A:** Five. In order: Naples-Marco Island (2), Vero Beach (4), Cape Coral-Ft. Myers (5), St. Lucie-Ft. Pierce (6), Punta Gorda (9).

53. **Q:** What fraction of U.S.'s new golf courses built in 2003 was in Florida?
    **A:** It was 15.5 18-hole equivalents out of 171.

54. **Q:** Sarasota claims to be the American birthplace of what sport?
    **A:** Golf. The game was introduced in the area in 1888.

55. **Q:** Where will you find golf's "blue monster"?
    **A:** It's the Doral Resort and Country Club in suburban Miami. The course is considered the most challenging on the Professional Golfers Association (PGA) tour.

56. **Q:** What sporting event in Jacksonville between "Gentleman Jim" Corbett and Charles Mitchell did soldiers try to stop on January 23, 1894?
    **A:** An illegal boxing match. The mayor and governor, morally opposed to the blood sport, had ordered the match called off, but promoters wouldn't budge. British challenger Mitchell was arrested on his arrival, but posted bond. A local lawyer stopped an injunction, and the militia backed off. The fight went on in a blinding rain; Corbett won in a knockout. Criminal charges against both men failed to stick.

57. **Q:** What great boxing upset took place on February 25, 1964, in the Miami Beach Convention Hall?
    **A:** Cassius Clay—later Muhammad Ali—knocked out Sonny Liston in the seventh round for the heavyweight title. The 22-year-old Clay would go on to win two more heavyweight titles.

58. **Q:** What sport played mostly in South Florida, was founded in Spain's Basque region and uses a rock-hard ball that travels at up to 150 m.p.h.?
    **A:** Jai-alai. The Miami fronton (arena) is the oldest and largest in the country.

59. **Q:** What water sport injects $1 billion a year into Florida's economy?
    **A:** Underwater diving.

60. **Q:** Where does Florida rank in the world as an underwater diving destination?
    **A:** First.

61. **Q:** Florida hosts what fraction of the world's divers every year?
    **A:** One-third.

62. **Q:** What is signified by a red flag floating in the ocean with a diagonal white stripe from upper left to lower right?
    **A:** It tells boaters that divers are in the area and caution should be exercised.

63. **Q:** What do sports divers get to hunt for 48 hours every summer before the commercial season starts?
    **A:** Lobsters.

Sports divers get a head start on tasty Florida lobsters. (*Miami News*)

64. **Q:** What underwater television series of the 1960s was filmed in north central Florida's Silver Springs?
**A:** *Sea Hunt.*

Loyd Bridges brought underwater diving to the TV screen.

65. **Q:** What inland water sport kills about a half dozen people in Florida every year?
**A:** Cave diving. Inexperienced or careless divers can get lost in the maze of underwater caves and run out of air.

66. **Q:** What water sport has an international museum in Panama City?
**A:** Underwater diving. Exhibits display the activity's 5,000-year history. The museum, opened in 1982, is operated by the non-profit Institute of Diving, founded in 1976 by a group that included veterans of the U.S. Navy's SEALAB program.

67. **Q:** What water sport has its national headquarters and a museum and hall of fame in Winter Haven?
**A:** Water skiing.

68. **Q:** What water sport has an international hall of fame in Fort Lauderdale?
**A:** Swimming. The 2-story building just off State Road A1A has an Olympic-size pool.

69. **Q:** Islamorada claims to be the world's capital for what sport?
**A:** Sportfishing.

70. **Q:** Why do dozens of people drive 200 times around a circle in North Florida every February?
**A:** For the Daytona 500, one of America's premiere stock car races. The 2-1/2 mile track at Daytona International Speedway is second only to Indianapolis in racing fame.

71. **Q:** What would happen if a car slowed to below 60 m.p.h. on one of the curves at Daytona International Speedway?
**A:** The high-banked curves are so steep the cars must stay above 60 to keep from falling off them.

72. **Q:** What 12-hour-long internationally-famous sporting event takes place every year at the airport in Sebring?
**A:** The 12 Hours of Sebring Endurance Race.

73. **Q:** Between 1902 and 1935, 13 speed records for what mode of transportation fell at Daytona Beach?
**A:** Automobiles. The 500-foot-wide (at low tide) beaches at Daytona Beach were perfect for speed racing.

74. **Q:** What stadium in Florida holds 167,785 people?
**A:** Daytona International Speedway.

75. **Q:** What are Stetson college teams called?
**A:** The Hatters. The college in DeLand was founded in 1886 by the head of the Stetson hat company.

## THE FLORIDA MARLINS

The Florida Marlins began play in 1993 (Florida Marlins)

**76. Q:** What sports event happened on April 5, 1993, for the first time ever in Florida?
**A:** Under a bright blue sky, Florida's first major league baseball team, the Florida Marlins, played its first regular season game. The Marlins were unlikely World Series champions in 1997 and 2003.

**77. Q:** What was the South Florida connection of Charlie Hough, who threw the first pitch of the Florida Marlins' historic first regular season game on April 5, 1993?
**A:** Hough grew up in nearby Hialeah.

**78. Q:** Who won the Florida Marlins' first game?
**A:** The Marlins went into the win column, beating the Los Angeles Dodgers 6-3 and starting the franchise in first place. Being an expansion team, it didn't last; the Marlins ended their first season 64-98.

**79. Q:** In what stadium does the Florida Marlins baseball team play?
**A:** The former Joe Robbie, now Pro Player, Stadium. Then-Marlins owner Wayne Huzeinga spent about $30 million to make the stadium home of his National Football League Miami Dolphins convertible for both sports.

**80. Q:** In 1993, Florida started up its second franchise in what un-Floridian major league sport?
**A:** Hockey. The Florida Panthers' first regular season game was October 6, 1993. The Tampa Bay Lightning began play in 1992. While critics wondered if hockey could work in sunny Florida, supporters argued it had a huge potential fan base in the state's large population of part-time and permanent residents from the northern United States and Canada.

**81. Q:** What major professional sports franchise in Florida was born on November 30, 1993?
**A:** The Jacksonville Jaguars of the National Football League. The team was to start play in 1995.

**82. Q:** With the creation of the Jacksonville Jaguars, how does Florida rank among states with the most NFL franchises?
**A:** Florida's three franchises (Miami, Tampa, Jacksonville) tie it with California (San Diego, San Francisco, Los Angeles.) New York technically has three but only the Buffalo Bills play in the state; the Giants and Jets play in New Jersey. States with two teams: Missouri (Kansas City, St. Louis) Ohio (Cleveland, Cincinnati), Pennsylvania (Philadelphia, Pittsburgh) and Texas (Dallas and Houston).

# 7
# *Let Me Entertain You*

1. **Q:** Jacksonville was, for a time, the national center for what entertainment industry?
   **A:** Film-making. At the turn of the century, film makers looking for a warm climate came to Jacksonville, and for a while it was "The World's Winter Film Capital." From 1912 to 1914, there were more working film companies in Jacksonville and St. Augustine than in Los Angeles. But the people of Jacksonville, who saw the business as unseemly, discouraged its settlement and it eventually moved to California.

2. **Q:** What half of one of filmdom's greatest comedy duos made many films in Jacksonville in the 1910s and 1920s?
   **A:** Oliver Hardy, of Laurel and Hardy fame.

3. **Q:** What series of early action films was shot in the clear waters of Wakulla Springs, south of Tallahassee?
   **A:** *Tarzan*, starring Johnny Weismuller.

4. **Q:** The famous boat from what Humphrey Bogart movie can be seen in Key Largo?
   **A:** *The African Queen.*

5. **Q:** What Humphrey Bogart film was based in the Florida Keys?
   **A:** *Key Largo.*

The boat used in *The African Queen* is on display in Key Largo.

Oliver Hardy (right), of Laurel and Hardy fame, made many films in Florida. (PBS-TV)

44

6. **Q:** What budget horror classic was shot in Wakulla Springs, south of Tallahassee?
**A:** *Creature from the Black Lagoon.*

7. **Q:** A chase scene from what super-spy movie series was filmed on the north fork of the St. Lucie River near Stuart?
**A:** James Bond's *Moonraker.*

8. **Q:** What film featuring alien beings, giant pods at the ocean bottom, and a geriatric break dancer was filmed in 1986 in the St. Petersburg area?
**A:** *Cocoon.* Don Ameche's break-dancing scene was filmed at the Coliseum, a historic dance hall with a 13,000-square-foot maple dance floor.

9. **Q:** What infamous pornographic film was shot in six days in Fort Lauderdale, Miami, and Coral Gables at a cost of only $24,000?
**A:** *Deep Throat.*

10. **Q:** What film featuring comedian Steve Martin and his fictional family was one of the first filmed at the Disney-MGM studios in Orlando?
**A:** *Parenthood.*

11. **Q:** What 1960s television programs featured a dolphin and a bear, respectively, and were produced in South Florida?
**A:** *Flipper* and *Gentle Ben.*

Buddy Ebsen, famous as Jed Clampett, might have been the Tin Man. (USA Network)

12. **Q:** What cast member of the 1960s television series *The Beverly Hillbillies* attended the University of Florida?
**A:** Buddy Ebsen.

13. **Q:** In what famous movie role was former University of Florida student Buddy Ebsen selected, then rejected?
**A:** The Tin Man in *The Wizard of Oz.* Ebsen had to pull out early in filming because the silver paint made him ill.

14. **Q:** What television cop show put Miami on the map when it debuted in the fall of 1984?
**A:** *Miami Vice.*

*Miami Vice* spotlighted the city's good and bad. (NBC-TV)

*Flipper* was shot in South Florida. (NBC-TV)

**15. Q:** What kind of playing takes place at the Coconut Grove Playhouse?
**A:** Theatrical plays. The historic building dates back to the 1920s.

**16. Q:** Florida State University is the only college in the country that puts on what kind of big show?
**A:** A circus. The FSU Flying High Circus was founded in 1946.

The FSU Flying High Circus was founded in 1946.

**17. Q:** What was completely dismantled in 1930 and moved to Sarasota, where it became part of an official state institution?
**A:** The entire interior of an 19th-century playhouse was taken apart in 1930 in Asolo, Italy, near Venice, stored for 20 years, and eventually bought by the state of Florida and moved to Sarasota. The 300-seat facility later housed Florida's official state theater; a new Asolo was later built across the street.

**18. Q:** What did Jim Morrison of the rock group The Doors do on stage at Dinner Key Auditorium on March 1, 1969, that got him arrested?
**A:** The Melbourne, Fla., native exposed himself during a concert. Morrison later surrendered in Los Angeles to charges of interstate flight to avoid prosecution. He was convicted on the indecency charge but appealed the case, which had not been resolved when Morrison drowned at age 27 in a Paris bathtub on July 3, 1971.

**19. Q:** When Jim Morrison of the rock group The Doors exposed himself at a 1969 Miami concert, the incident spurred 30,000 people to gather at the Orange Bowl for what?
**A:** A "rally for decency" that featured entertainer Jackie Gleason and singer Anita Bryant, who years later would fight a Dade County referendum giving rights to gays.

**20. Q:** What rock star who appeared at Woodstock grew up in Central Florida?
**A:** Steven Stills attended the Admiral Farragut Military Academy in St. Petersburg, then moved through public and private schools and got involved in garage bands, playing dates ranging from University of Florida fraternity parties in Gainesville to proms in Palatka. He attended the university for only six weeks.

Central Florida's Stephen Stills became a rock legend.

**21. Q:** What Florida city hosted a rock concert 3-1/2 months after Woodstock that drew 40,000 people?
**A:** Like its famous cousin, the First Annual Palm Beach International Music and Arts Festival, November 28-30, 1969, had problems. A cold rain turned the site northwest of West Palm Beach into a quagmire. Everything ran late; the last act, the Rolling Stones, appeared near dawn the last day. Two decades later, the sheriff admitted he had his men dig up fire ant piles and move them to the site and tried to encourage alligators to enter nearby canals, all in an effort to disrupt the event or push fans into leaving early. Among the acts: Rolling Stones, Grand Funk Railroad, Janis Joplin, Iron Butterfly, Vanilla Fudge, Jefferson Airplane, and Sly and the Family Stone.

**22. Q:** What legendary southern rock group started in Daytona Beach?
**A:** The Allman Brothers, born in Tennessee, moved to Daytona Beach as youngsters and got their start playing the tourist town's youth clubs.

**23. Q:** Several members of what Jacksonville-based rock group were killed in a plane crash in Mississippi on October 20, 1977?
**A:** Lynyrd Skynyrd.

**24. Q:** For whom was the Jacksonville-based rock group Lynyrd Skynyrd named?
**A:** Their high school coach, Leonard Skinner, who constantly harassed them for their long hair and manners.

**25. Q:** What reggae superstar died in Miami on May 11, 1980?
**A:** Bob Marley died of cancer in a Miami hospital. He was 36.

**26. Q:** What rock-and-roll star grew up in Gainesville?
**A:** Tom Petty.

**27. Q:** What Latin rock super-group has a Florida city in its name?
**A:** Gloria Estefan and Miami Sound Machine.

Gloria Estefan

# 8
# *People*

1. **Q:** Which famous western writer wrote while vacationing at Layton, in the Florida Keys?
   **A:** Zane Grey. The writer was also president of the Long Key Fishing Club.

**PAPA IN FLORIDA**

2. **Q:** Who wrote, drank, fished and lived the tropical lifestyle at his home at 907 Whitehead Street in Key West?
   **A:** Ernest Hemingway. It was there he wrote *Death in the Afternoon, Green Hills of Africa,* and *To Have and Have Not* and began *For Whom the Bell Tolls.* The home, built in 1851, is now a historic landmark.

Ernest Hemingway and his cats in Key West (Scribners Publishing)

Hemingway's Key West home is now a museum. (Florida Keys & Key West Visitors Bureau)

3. **Q:** What unusual animals can be found at the Key West home of writer Ernest Hemingway?
   **A:** Six-toed cats said to be descendants of Hemingway's pets.

4. **Q:** After poet Wallace Stevens criticized Ernest Hemingway's works to his sister at a party in Key West, how did Hemingway react?

   **A:** He stormed into the party, called Stevens outside, and broke his jaw with a single right hook. Both men would later win Pulitzer Prizes and Hemingway a Nobel Prize.

5. **Q:** What sporting events did Ernest Hemingway referee in Key West in the 1930s?
   **A:** Friday night open-arena boxing matches.

Marjorie Kinnan Rawlings wrote of rustic Cross Creek, in North Florida. (University of Florida)

**6.** **Q:** What tale of a rural North Florida boy, his pet fawn, and his transition into manhood won a Pulitzer Prize in 1939?
**A:** Marjorie Kinnan Rawlings' *The Yearling.*

Marjory Stoneman Douglas (PBS)

**7.** **Q:** Who lived longer: North Florida author Marjorie Kinnan Rawlings or South Florida writer and environmentalist Marjory Stoneman Douglas?
**A:** Rawlings died in 1953 at 57. Douglas died in May 1998 at age 108.

**8.** **Q:** What north central Florida settlement did author Marjorie Kinnan Rawlings make her home and immortalize in her books?
**A:** *Cross Creek.*

**9.** **Q:** What imaginary detective docked his boat, *The Busted Flush,* at slip F-18 at the Bahia Mar marina in Fort Lauderdale?
**A:** Travis McGee, the creation of Sarasota resident John D. MacDonald, who died in 1986, at 70.

**10.** **Q:** What do the titles of the 21 Travis McGee novels have in common?
**A:** They all mention a color.

**11.** **Q:** In order to do detailed illustrations of Florida's unusual wildlife, famed naturalist John James Audubon did something to the animals that would shock his followers. What did he do?
**A:** He killed them so he could study them closely for the drawings.

**12.** **Q:** A museum to what eclectic mustachioed modern painter is in St. Petersburg?
**A:** Salvador Dali. The museum has the world's largest collection of works by the Spanish surrealist, who died at 84 in 1989. The collection, valued at about $100 million, spans more than 60 years of Dali's work, from 1914 to 1980.

**13.** **Q:** Which rock-and-roll legend came to the northern Gulf coast town of Yankeetown—population then 425—in the summer of 1961 to film a movie?
**A:** Elvis Presley came to shoot his ninth film, *Follow That Dream.*

A young Elvis filmed *Follow That Dream* in Florida. (The Nashville Network)

Mel Tillis hails from the Lake Okeechobee area.

**14.** **Q:** What famous stuttering country singer is from the Lake Okeechobee town of Pahokee?
**A:** Mel Tillis.

15. **Q:** What Florida town did Caribbean balladeer Jimmy Buffett live in and use as a source for many of his songs?
**A:** Key West.

Jimmy Buffett sang of the characters of Key West. (MCA Records)

16. **Q:** Singer Jimmy Buffett's souvenir shop in Key West is named for what imaginary island immortalized in a Buffett song?
**A:** Margaritaville.

17. **Q:** What movie and television star lives near Jupiter and played football for Florida State University?
**A:** Burt Reynolds.

18. **Q:** What business did actor Burt Reynolds open in Jupiter in 1979?
**A:** The Burt Reynolds Dinner Theatre attracted major stars, brought affordable legitimate theater to South Floridians, and gave up-and-comers invaluable on-the-job training. The 449-seat theater's big budget and little ticket prices doomed it; in 1989, Reynolds sold it.

19. **Q:** What Hollywood starlet came from the tiny Panhandle town of Bascom and attended the University of Florida and Florida State University before becoming famous for playing a gangster and a television executive?
**A:** Faye Dunaway, who starred in *Bonnie and Clyde* and won an Oscar for *Network*.

20. **Q:** How many "Miss Floridas" have won the "Miss America" pageant?
**A:** Two. The first one, Leanza Cornett, won in 1992. Ericka

Dunlap won in 2003.

21. **Q:** Which star of the popular television sitcom *Designing Women* was "Miss Florida" in 1974?
**A:** Delta Burke represented Orlando.

Delta Burke was a "Miss Florida" (CBS-TV)

22. **Q:** What actor and suntan legend attended Palm Beach High School in 1957?
**A:** George Hamilton.

23. **Q:** What black actor, raised in Miami, made film history by coming to dinner?
**A:** Sidney Poitier. In the 1967 movie *Guess Who's Coming to Dinner?*, Spencer Tracy and Katherine Hepburn—it was his last film; she won an Oscar—are shocked when their daughter brings home her black fiancé.

24. **Q:** What half of one of America's most beloved comedy couples attended Miami High School?
**A:** Desi Arnaz. The Cuban-born musician also attended St. Patrick's, a Miami Beach Catholic school.

Desi Arnaz in 1940 (RKO pictures)

**25. Q:** Bob Smith, who later retired to Fort Lauderdale, was once the most famous sidekick in television. Who was his foil?
**A:** In the 1950s, every kid in America knew what time it was: "It's Howdy Doody Time!" Buffalo Bob Smith and his puppet friend were household names. The television show is now part of history, and Smith died in 1998.

**26. Q:** What radio personality did many of his shows from Miami Beach and has a street there named for him?
**A:** Arthur Godfrey.

**27. Q:** What comedy superstar broadcast his shows in the 1960s from Miami Beach, praised in the show's opening as "The Sun and Fun Capital of the World?"
**A:** Jackie Gleason. He later retired to South Florida, where he died in 1987.

Howdy Doody and Buffalo Bob retired to Fort Lauderdale.

The Great One, Jackie Gleason, in 1969.

**28. Q:** What's the home town of Esther Rolle, famous as television maid "Florida" in the shows *Maude* and *Good Times*?
**A:** Pompano Beach.

**29. Q:** What broadcasting magnate owns an exotic animal ranch in the small Panhandle town of Capps?
**A:** Ted Turner, owner of Cable News Network.

**30. Q:** What world-prominent preacher was baptized as a young man in Silver Lake, west of Palatka, in 1942?
**A:** Billy Graham. He heard "the call" while a student at Florida Bible Institute in the Tampa suburb of Temple Terrace. After graduating in 1940, he began preaching to skid row bums and drunks from a Tampa sidewalk. He is believed to have preached to millions—more than any person.

**31. Q:** What recently retired female tennis superstar grew up in Fort Lauderdale and now lives in Boca Raton?
**A:** Chris Evert.

**32. Q:** What Romanian Olympic superstar defected to South Florida in December 1989?
**A:** Nadia Comaneci.

**33. Q:** What part-time job did colorful Key West bar owner "Captain Tony" Tarracino take on in November 1989?
**A:** Mayor. Local residents, fearful that development was destroying their town's eclectic, laid-back beauty,

elected the 73-year-old one-time fisherman, treasure hunter, and casino operator on an anti-development platform. Tarracino failed in a 1991 reelection bid.

34. **Q:** What co-founder of Standard Oil spent his twilight years in Ormond Beach, trying desperately to reach the age of 100?
**A:** John D. Rockefeller Sr. died in 1937, at the age of 97.

John D. Rockefeller in 1930, seven years before his death. (P&A Photos)

35. **Q:** While living out his twilight years in Ormond Beach, what did multimillionaire John D. Rockefeller hand out to children outside his church every Sunday?
**A:** He handed dimes to youngsters to teach them thrift. But each year, as he headed back north at the end of the winter, it is said he handed the pastor an envelope paying all the church's expenses for the coming year.

36. **Q:** Carl Fisher, who later founded Miami Beach, also created the venue for what world-famous sporting event?
**A:** Indianapolis Motor Speedway, home of the Indianapolis 500.

37. **Q:** In the early part of the 20th century, one man owned 1.3 million acres of southwest Florida, covering nearly

all of the present Collier County and parts of other counties. What was his name?
**A:** Collier, of course—land baron Barron Collier. That 1.3 million acres is an area bigger than Delaware.

38. **Q:** What's the name of developer Henry Flagler's former home in Palm Beach, now a museum?
**A:** Whitehall. The mansion was built in 1902, for $4 million.

39. **Q:** Where is famed Florida developer Henry Flagler buried?
**A:** Not in Miami, the tiny settlement he put on the map, nor in Palm Beach, which he made synonymous with Florida high society and where his mansion is now a museum. Flagler lies beside his first wife, Mary, in a mausoleum at a church in St. Augustine, his original tourist mecca in Florida.

40. **Q:** Sarasota's palatial "Ca' d'Zan" was the home of what national entertainment figure?
**A:** The "House of John," completed in the mid-1920s, was home of circus magnate John Ringling, of Ringling Brothers fame. His home and an adjoining art museum are now owned by the state.

41. **Q:** According to legend, how did circus magnate and Sarasota pioneer John Ringling obtain popular St. Armand's Key?
**A:** He supposedly won the island in a poker game.

42. **Q:** Who is buried in William Brickell's mausoleum in downtown Miami?
**A:** No one. Brickell died in 1908, his wife in 1922. In 1948, his daughter removed their bodies to a Miami cemetery because she decided downtown Miami had become too noisy.

# THOMAS EDISON: THE WIZARD IN FLORIDA

**43. Q:** What famous inventor wintered in Fort Myers?
**A:** Thomas Edison. The inventor used the home and laboratory at "Seminole Lodge" from 1885 to his death in 1931, and his widow donated the home to the city in 1947. It is now a historic site and museum.

**44. Q:** What technological feat did inventor Thomas Edison offer to do for the city of Fort Myers?
**A:** Officials turned down his offer to construct a power plant to light the city. They cited the expense of light poles and feared the light would keep cows awake.

**45. Q:** What auto pioneer had a winter home next door to Thomas Edison's in Fort Myers?
**A:** Henry Ford. The car-making giant's Fort Myers estate was bought by the city in 1988 as a historic site.

**46. Q:** How much was auto magnate Henry Ford II, grandson of the motor company's founder, worth when the Palm Beach resident died in 1987?
**A:** Probate records showed he left an estate of about $250 million.

**47. Q:** Which former astronaut ran the now-defunct Eastern Airlines?
**A:** Frank Borman.

**48. Q:** What famous flyer flew into oblivion from an airport near Miami on June 1, 1937?

Amelia Earhart disappeared in 1937.

**A:** Amelia Earhart began her last flight from the airport. She disappeared over the Pacific Ocean July 3, 1937.

**49. Q:** What fate befell George End, who set up a rattlesnake meat canning operation and tourist stand in the 1930s on the Gandy Bridge from Tampa to St. Petersburg?
**A:** End, co-founder of the community called Rattlesnake, was fatally bitten by one of his snakes.

**50. Q:** What famous gangster lived at 10 Palm Avenue on Palm Island, near Miami Beach?
**A:** Al Capone paid $40,000 in 1930 for "Casa Contenta"—now worth $1 million to $1.8 million.

**51. Q:** How did Panama City drifter Clarence Gideon, convicted of robbing a pool hall, later make legal history?
**A:** His appeal led to the March 18, 1963, *Gideon v. Wainright* U.S. Supreme Court decision that the accused have the right to a lawyer even if they can't afford one.

Gideon was retried and acquitted. He died in Fort Lauderdale in 1972.

52. **Q:** What happened to Barbara Jane Mackle, daughter of a wealthy Miami developer, in an Atlanta hotel room on Dec. 17, 1968?
**A:** She was kidnapped by two men. She was later buried alive in the Georgia countryside for 83 hours before being rescued by the FBI.

53. **Q:** What's the name of the major who established a fort along the New River in present-day Broward County during the Second Seminole War?
**A:** Major William Lauderdale, who founded Fort Lauderdale.

54. **Q:** When "Uncle Bill" Lundy died in 1957 in Crestview at the reported age of 109, he was claimed to be Florida's oldest veteran of what part of American history?
**A:** The Civil War.

55. **Q:** Until Neno Feagle died in a Lake City nursing home at age 91 on April 22, 1985, she was Florida's last surviving widow of what war?
**A:** The Civil War.

Mary McCleod Bethune was a pioneer in education. (United Methodist Communications)

56. **Q:** What did black pioneer Mary McLeod Bethune found in 1904 in a dilapidated cabin in Daytona Beach?
**A:** A small school for daughters of railroad workers that has grown to Bethune-Cookman College.

57. **Q:** For whom is the Keys-based Radio Martí and Television Martí named?
**A:** The U.S. government's Caribbean version of Radio Free Europe, which beamed programming into Cuba, was named for José Martí, the man who helped spark the ouster of colonial Spain from the island nation.

# 9
# *Politics*

1.  **Q:** How many capitals has Florida
    had since statehood?
    **A:** Just one: Tallahassee, although
    towns like Orlando and Miami
    have been suggested as Florida
    has become more bottom-heavy in
    population.

2.  **Q:** Was Pensacola ever a capital
    of Florida?
    **A:** Only the territory of West
    Florida—which included parts of
    Alabama, Mississippi, and
    Louisiana—before it was shrunk
    and combined with East Florida.

3.  **Q:** What was Florida's capital
    before Tallahassee?
    **A:** St. Augustine for East Florida
    and Pensacola for West Florida.
    When the territories merged, the
    centrally-located Tallahassee was
    selected as the new capital.

4.  **Q:** Before Tallahassee was selected,
    state officials briefly alternated
    government business between
    Pensacola and St. Augustine, but
    the long trip between cities
    spurred the call for a central cap-
    ital. How long did the trip take?
    **A:** Twenty days.

5.  **Q:** In 1900, Florida voters defeated
    a proposal to move the state cap-
    ital from Tallahassee to a more
    central location. Which three cities
    were rejected?
    **A:** Ocala, St. Augustine, and
    Jacksonville.

6.  **Q:** What effort by state senator Lee
    Weissenborn is sarcastically hon-
    ored with a plaque in the new
    state capitol in Tallahassee?
    **A:** Weissenborn's efforts to move
    the capital to the more central
    Orlando spurred the building of
    the new state capitol building in
    the late 1970s.

7.  **Q:** What did John E. Matthews do
    for 7-3/4 hours on May 28, 1931,
    in Tallahassee?
    **Q:** He set a one-day filibuster
    record during a 19-hour talkathon
    that ended in a Matthews win and
    a fistfight on the floor of the Florida
    House of Representatives.

8.  **Q:** What political distinction does
    tiny Indian Key hold?
    **A:** Miami is the Dade County seat
    now, but the first county seat—
    established February 4, 1836—was this
    island, still accessible only by boat
    and now a state park.

Indian Key was the first seat of Dade County. (Florida Keys & Key West Visitors Bureau)

9.  **Q:** What community became the only incorporated city on the east coast south of St. Augustine on July 28, 1896?
    **A:** When Miami was born, only 343 votes were cast, but that was still more than the 312 registered voters who gathered over a pool hall to vote. Hmmm.

10. **Q:** Have any of Florida's 67 counties have been formed in this century?
    **A:** Yes, 20 of them, all between 1911 and 1925. Gilchrist is the last county formed in Florida; it came into being on December 4, 1925.

11. **Q:** In 1886, the Florida Senate approved and sent to the house a constitutional amendment that would have officially denied the right to vote to whom?
    **A:** Blacks, women and people under 21. The law would have given the right to vote only to "white male persons, of the age of 21 years and upward." The U.S. Constitution, in its 15th

Amendment, had already guaranteed blacks the vote in 1870 and the 19th Amendment, ratified in 1920, included women. In 1971, the 26th Amendment lowered the voting age to 18.

12. **Q:** What did Mrs. Fay Bridges do in the Panhandle town of Sneads on Aug. 27, 1920, that no woman had ever done in Florida?
    **A:** She voted. Mrs. Bridges cast ballots for mayor and constable on the porch of the general store where she worked. One day earlier, the state's secretary of state had proclaimed ratification of the 19th Amendment to the U.S. Constitution.

13. **Q:** From what demographic group was Rhonda Spence the first ever to vote in Florida when she cast her ballot on July 13, 1971, in the Panhandle town of DeFuniak Springs?
    **A:** Spence, a 20-year-old student, was the first person under 21 to vote in an election. She was one of 66 people between 18 and 20 qualified to vote for three city councilmen.

Florida state senate, 1889. (Florida Photographic Archives)

**14. Q:** In 1891 the Florida House of Representatives passed a resolution permitting the expulsion from its chambers of people of what occupation?

**A:** Journalists. The resolution said merely a charge of unfair coverage by a legislator was enough to have a correspondent booted.

**15. Q:** Before the 17th Amendment to the U.S. Constitution, how did Floridians get their U.S. senators?

**A:** The position was filled by the state legislature.

**16. Q:** How were Florida's U.S. senators picked in the mid-1800s?

**A:** State legislators drew lots.

**17. Q:** What two political positions were held by the same two people for much of the first one-third of the 20th century?

**A:** Duncan U. Fletcher and Park Trammell were U.S. senators from Florida; Fletcher from 1914 to 1936 and Trammell from 1917 to 1936.

**18. Q:** Why did both Florida U.S. Senate positions suddenly come open within about six weeks of each other in 1936, forcing special elections?

**A:** Duncan U. Fletcher and Park Trammell both died; Trammell on May 8 and Fletcher on June 17.

## CLAUDE PEPPER, FLORIDA'S ELDER STATESMAN

**19. Q:** What was Ronald Reagan doing when Congressman Claude Pepper, who died in May 1989 at the age of 88, won his first elected office?

**A:** Pepper was elected to the Florida legislature in 1928, when the future president was in middle school.

**20. Q:** For what high office did Claude Pepper make a brief bid in 1948?

**A:** Then-U.S. Senator Pepper failed to persuade World War II hero Dwight Eisenhower to run on the Democratic ticket, so he offered himself. Incumbent Harry Truman beat favored Republican Thomas Dewey that year in one of America's greatest election upsets. Eisenhower was elected on the Republican ticket four years later.

**21. Q:** In 1950, George Smathers reportedly called Claude Pepper "an extrovert" who practiced "nepotism with his sister- in-law," whose sister was "a thespian," and who "practiced celibacy" before his marriage. What event prompted the alleged doubletalk?

**A:** It was the U.S. Senate Democratic primary, considered one of the ugliest on record. Naive rural voters were supposedly horrified and Smathers beat incumbent Pepper. No one has ever seen documentation for the incident and many historians now doubt it occurred.

22. **Q:** In 1968, Ed Gurney became the first Republican in Florida ever elected to what office?
**A:** U.S. senator.

Lawton Chiles became U.S. Senator in 1970 and governor 20 years later.

23. **Q:** What gimmick did Lawton Chiles employ in 1970 while running for the U.S. Senate?
**A:** The obscure state senator from Lakeland walked across Florida to introduce himself to the people. It worked, leading to an 18-year term in Washington. He later came out of retirement and was elected governor in 1990. He died in office in 1998.

24. **Q:** What was the significance of Richard Stone's election to the U.S. Senate from Florida in 1974?
**A:** Stone was the first Jew ever elected to the U.S. Senate from a southern state by popular vote.

25. **Q:** In the 1986 Florida U.S. Senate race, Democrat Bob Graham and Republican Paula Hawkins combined to spend $12.6 million. To what amount were candidates limited in the 1913 race?
**A:** They could spend no more than $4,000 each.

26. **Q:** What U.S. senator, elected in 1988, was the grandson of a famous baseball manager?
**A:** Connie Mack III. The resident of Cape Coral, near Fort Myers, is grandson of Connie Mack, who managed and owned the Philadelphia Athletics. The senator's father was one of the founders of Cape Coral.

27. **Q:** What was the closest U.S. Senate race in Florida history?
**A:** In 1988, Republican Connie Mack beat Democrat Buddy MacKay with 50.2 percent of the vote.

28. **Q:** On November 6, 1868, Jonathan Gibbs was appointed Secretary of State, becoming the state's first-ever cabinet member from what minority?
**A:** He was the first black cabinet member.

29. **Q:** Who was the first Republican governor since Reconstruction?
**A:** Claude Kirk, elected on Nov. 8, 1966.

30. **Q:** On November 5, 1974, Reubin Askew became the first Florida governor with what distinction?
**A:** He was the first ever elected to a second term.

31. **Q:** Why did Bob Graham do a different job every day in 1977 and 1978?
**A:** The little-known state senator from Miami Lakes used 108 "workdays," in jobs ranging from trash collector at a county fair to writer at an all-news radio station, to draw attention in his bid for governor. It worked.

Bob Graham, busboy, conducts one of his workdays in 1977 in his campaign for govenor. (*Miami News*)

32. **Q:** What was the occupation of 16 of the 23 governors elected in the 20th century?
    **A:** Lawyer.

33. **Q:** What precedent was set by Bob Martinez' election as governor in 1986?
    **A:** He was the state's first-ever Hispanic governor.

34. **Q:** Wayne Mixson served the shortest term ever as Florida governor. How long was his term?
    **A:** Three days. Mixson, lieutenant governor under Bob Graham, took over the office on January 3, 1987, because Graham, recently elected U.S. senator, started his new job three days before his old one expired. Mixson, 64, later turned the office over to incoming governor Bob Martinez.

35. **Q:** On November 12, 1985, Xavier Suarez became Miami's first-ever mayor born in what country?
    **A:** Cuba.

36. **Q:** On November 6, 1973, Maurice Ferre was elected Miami's first mayor from what minority?
    **A:** He was the city's first Hispanic mayor.

Maurice Ferre (Miami-Metro Department of Publicity and Tourism)

37. **Q:** In November 1951, a postcard was sent to then-president Harry Truman, on one of his several vacations in Key West. What happened?
    **A:** Although addressed to the president of the United States, it was returned to the sender for insufficient address.

38. **Q:** A son of what former president was mayor of Miami Beach in the 1960s?
    **A:** Elliot Roosevelt, son of Franklin D. Roosevelt.

## JOHN F. KENNEDY: CAMELOT'S FLORIDA HOME

39. **Q:** What politician made stops in Miami and Tampa in 1963 just days before he was slain?
    **A:** On November 19, 1963, President John F. Kennedy made appearances in Miami and Tampa before heading to Dallas.

40. **Q:** Where did President John F. Kennedy spend the last Sunday of his life?
    **A:** At his family home in Palm Beach.

41. **Q:** What Florida facility was named for John F. Kennedy 10 days after he last visited it?
    **A:** Cape Kennedy, now the Kennedy Space Center at Cape Canaveral.

John. F. Kennedy spent the last weekend of his life in Florida. (Kennedy Library)

## RICHARD NIXON IN FLORIDA

Richard Nixon, nominated at the 1968 GOP convention in Miami Beach. (*Miami News*)

**42. Q:** What happened to Richard Nixon in Miami Beach on August 5, 1968, and again on July 11, 1972?
**A:** The nation's 37th president received both his nominations at Republican conventions held in Miami Beach.

**43. Q:** In 1973, the "Gainesville Eight" were acquitted of trying to disrupt what 1972 event in Miami Beach?
**A:** The Republican National Convention.

**44. Q:** Where did Richard Nixon say "I am not a crook" on November 17, 1973?
**A:** He made his famous remark at a news conference at Walt Disney World.

**45. Q:** Where did Richard Nixon keep a vacation home when he was president?
**A:** Key Biscayne.

**46. Q:** What former Secretary of State and sometime presidential candidate has a home in Manalapan, south of Palm Beach?
**A:** Alexander Haig—chairman of the Joint Chiefs of Staff during the Nixon administration, commander of the North Atlantic Treaty Organization (NATO) in the 1970s, and President Ronald Reagan's Secretary of State. It was Haig who, after Reagan was shot in 1981, declared "I'm in charge now." Haig had a brief run for president in 1988.

**47. Q:** On November 20, 1975, in Miami, a prankster lunged at a Republican presidential candidate with a fake gun. The politician's next encounter with a gunman was for real. Who was the candidate?
**A:** Ronald Reagan, who lost in the 1976 bid but was elected in 1980. On March 30, 1981, Reagan was shot in the chest outside a Washington, D. C. hotel along with his press secretary, a policeman, and a Secret Service agent. All survived.

**48. Q:** In 1977, in a campaign led by entertainer and citrus industry spokeswoman Anita Bryant, voters turned down a Dade County ordinance that would have given equal rights to what group?
**A:** Homosexuals.

**49. Q:** The establishment of what pastime in Miami Beach was rejected by voters in 1978, 1986, and 1994?
**A:** Casino gambling.

50. **Q:** The presidential yacht *USS Sequoia*, which hosted nine chief executives over nearly five decades, was sold in 1977 and by 1980 was performing what function at a dock in Stuart?
**A:** It was a floating cocktail lounge. The boat was rescued from obscurity and after costly renovations, it was recommissioned in 1988.

51. **Q:** What is the building in Washington, D.C., called the "Florida House"?
**A:** It's a state "embassy." More than 250,000 Florida residents have used it to meet, get directions, and make hotel and travel arrangements. The renovated 1891 Victorian townhouse, a block north of the U.S. Capitol, was the idea of then-U.S. Senator Lawton Chiles and his wife, Rhea. It was bought in 1972 by Florida politicians and businessmen and opened the following year, and is maintained by contributions.

52. **Q:** What U.S. congressman from Florida rode in space?
**A:** Bill Nelson of Melbourne rode on the space shuttle in 1986.

# 10
# *Animal, Vegetable, Mineral*

1. **Q:** What tasty Florida sea animals are nicknamed "bugs?"
   **A.** Spiny lobsters.

2. **Q:** What have spiny lobsters been known to do off the Florida coast after a strong fall storm?
   **A:** When storms damage their habitat, a group of lobsters will line up single-file, perhaps in the hundreds or thousands, and march across the ocean floor to another site.

3. **Q:** To what animal family does the conch belong?
   **A:** Snails.

4. **Q:** From what part of Florida did the conch you eat in the Florida Keys probably come?
   **A:** It didn't; it probably came from the Bahamas or another island. Overfishing and growth have decimated Florida's conch population and harvesting has been banned.

5. **Q:** What delicious sea animal made Apalachicola famous?
   **A:** Oysters.

6. **Q:** What do you do with the rest of a stone crab after you remove its claw?

**A:** Throw it back. The animal can regenerate a new claw in a few years.

7. **Q:** Beaches along Florida's central and southeast coast are often crawling with baby loggerheads in the spring. What are loggerheads?
   **A:** An endangered species of turtle.

8. **Q:** What have deputies in helicopters spotted a few feet from the ankles of unsuspecting swimmers at sandbars off South Florida?
   **A:** Sharks.

Sharks have been seen just feet from the ankles of swimmers.
(Hank Meyer Associates)

62

9. Q: Collecting what part of sharks has become a popular pastime in Venice?
A: After sharks die and decompose, their teeth are left on the ocean bottom and eventually wash ashore.

10. Q: What kind of fish can walk?
A: The walking catfish can slither across land, breathe air, and stay out of water for hours.

## ALLIGATORS AND CROCODILES: THE BIG LIZARDS

Does rubbing an alligator's belly put it to sleep? Want to try? (Historical Museum of Southern Florida)

11. Q: According to Seminole legend, rubbing an alligator's belly would make it do what?
A: Go to sleep.

12. Q: Where did the name "alligator" originate?
A: Spanish explorers were unable to identify the massive reptiles and called them "el lagarto"—the lizard.

13: Q: How many alligators were believed killed in Florida between 1889 and 1894?
A: Two and a half million.

14. Q: Only about 500 of this rare reptile live in the United States, with most in South Florida. What are they?
A: Crocodiles.

15. Q: What animals did lonely sailors misidentify as humans, sparking the mermaid legend?
A: Manatees, believe it or not. The homely but lovable sea mammals can reach a length of 13 feet and weigh up to a ton and a half.

16. Q: How many manatees are believed to exist in Florida?
A: Only about 3,000 of the animals are believed left. The animal is listed as an endangered species, meaning it is in imminent danger of extinction.

17. Q: Blue Spring State Park, between Orlando and Daytona Beach, was the state's first sanctuary for what animal?
A: The manatee.

18. Q: The key deer population in the Florida Keys has fallen victim to development and many have been killed by motorists. What makes the animal different from other types of deer?
A: Its size; it's about as big as a large dog.

**19. Q:** Juan Ponce de León is credited with introducing what animal to Florida?
**A:** The cow. On his second expedition, in 1521, he brought Andalusia cattle, relatives of the Texas longhorns. They were the ancestors of Florida's booming beef industry.

**20. Q:** What endangered predator roams the Everglades?
**A:** The Florida panther. Development has decimated the range of this cousin to the mountain lion; fewer than 100 are believed to be left.

The noble Florida panther. (Florida Game and Fresh Water Fish Commission)

**21. Q:** What animals, weighing 100 to 600 pounds and averaging five to six feet, roam much of Florida, and may snatch your picnic basket?
**A:** Bears.

**22. Q:** In 1988, the Humane Society of the United States investigated an unusual performance based in McIntosh, near Gainesville, in which mules do what?
**A:** They dive 40 feet into an 8-foot-deep tank. The troupe owned seven diving mules.

Animal rights activists claimed the act was cruel. The manager of a Maryland fair said mules are so stubborn they would never jump unless they wanted to.

## CREEPY CRAWLIES

**23. Q:** For four decades, tourists flocked to an attraction south of Miami that featured what deadly reptile?
**A:** The Miami Serpentarium had thousands of poisonous snakes, which owner Bill Haast also milked for venom for snake-bite antidotes and research. Haast moved his research center to Utah in 1984 and brought it to Punta Gorda in 1990.

**24. Q:** How does Florida rank among states in number of species of snakes?
**A:** First.

**25. Q:** To what does the safety-conscious rhyme "red touch yellow, kill a fellow; red touch black, friend of Jack" refer?
**A:** The coral snake, deadliest in North America, has red rings bordering on yellow rings. The nonvenomous king snake's red rings border on black rings.

**26. Q:** What was removed from a Coconut Creek woman's toilet on May 26, 1989?
**A:** A 6-foot boa constrictor.

**27. Q:** What are love bugs doing when they smash into your car in the spring and summer, leaving a sticky mess that can damage the finish?
**A:** They are mating in mid-air.

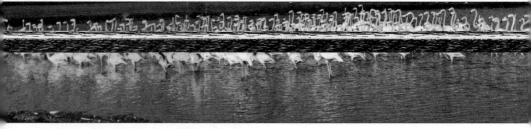

Flamingos grace Hialeah Race Track. (*Miami News*)

**28.** **Q:** Miami ranks first nationally in prevalence of what destructive household pest?
**A:** Termites.

**29.** **Q:** What animal has become a symbol for the Hialeah horse racing track and, for many people, Florida itself?
**A:** The flamingo. More than 400 live in the track's infield.

**30.** **Q:** Where in Florida will you find the West Indian monk seal?
**A:** Nowhere. The brownish-gray seal, about the size of a man, was noted by explorer Christopher Columbus in 1494, and was easy prey for hunters who coveted its meat and oil. The last known animal was killed in 1922.

**Q:** Where does Florida rank in number of endangered or threatened species?
**A:** It is second only to Hawaii.

**Q:** If you have key limes left over after you've made one of those famous pies, what else can you do with them?
**A:** Clean brass, make limeade, tenderize meat, substitute for vinegar in salad dressing, make sushi, whiten boiled rice, soften water, or remove stains.

**Q:** For what is Lignumvitae Key named?

**A:** The lignum vitae, a small native hardwood tree.

**34.** **Q:** How much of the Everglades did scientists fear the exotic melaleuca plant would overwhelm by the end of the 1990s?
**A:** About three-fourths. Introduced in 1906 from Australia as a timber source, it has no natural enemies in Florida. In 1990, scientists outlined a comprehensive $25 million battle plan that included chemicals, physical removal, and introduction of insects from Australia.

**35.** **Q:** In what peaceful central Florida town are 85 percent of the world's caladium flowers grown?
**A:** Lake Placid.

**36.** **Q:** Molesting what oceanside vegetation will net you a $50 fine?
**A:** Sea oats. The decorative tall perennial grasses are protected by state law. They have an extensive underground root system that binds sand and helps maintain beaches.

**37.** **Q:** What will you find near Sanford that is believed to be the oldest and largest of its kind in America?
**A:** "The Senator," a giant cypress tree 138 feet high and 47 feet around, with a diameter of 17-1/2 feet. It is believed to be 3,500 years old.

**38. Q:** What did diggers stumble across south of Miami that are believed to be among the oldest ever uncovered in North America?
**A:** Human remains were found in 1985 at a 10,000-year-old fossil site in Cutler Ridge—along with remains of prehistoric wolves, condors, and mammoths.

**39. Q:** What was found still inside 8,000-year-old human skulls in 1985 near Titusville?
**A:** Preserved brain material. Packed in peat, the brain matter was in such good shape that scientists were able to conduct DNA testing on it.

**40. Q:** Where did the Panhandle's brilliant white sand originate?
**A:** It started as rock material in the continent's interior that moved down to sea in rivers and streams.

**41. Q:** What luxury vehicle forms an artificial reef off Palm Beach?
**A:** A 1967 Silver Shadow Rolls Royce. The car, donated in September 1985, rests in 85 feet of water about one mile southeast of the Palm Beach inlet.

**42. Q:** What historic distinction is held by the Pelican Island National Wildlife Refuge, near Sebastian?
**A:** It was America's first national wildlife refuge, founded March 14, 1903.

**43. Q:** How many national wildlife refuges are in the Keys?
**A:** Four: Crocodile Lake, Key Deer, Great White Heron, and Key West.

A family enjoys the Corkscrew Swamp Sanctuary (Florida News Bureau)

**44. Q:** What conservation group owns and runs the Corkscrew Swamp Sanctuary east of Naples?
**A:** The National Audubon Society.

**45. Q:** The National Audubon Society runs a center for what kind of animal near Orlando?
**A:** Birds of prey.

**46. Q:** How does Florida rank among the states in number of bald eagles?
**A:** With about 2,000, it's second only to Alaska, with about 30,000.

# 11
# *Science, Weather and the Environment*

1. **Q:** For what did Apalachicola doctor John Gorrie receive a patent on May 6, 1851?
**A:** An ice-making machine. Now used most to cool beverages, it was originally designed to control the area's malaria epidemic.

Cold air pioneer John Gorrie.
(Florida State Archives)

2. **Q:** What did archaeologists use NASA technology to find in an Alachua County field in 1988?
**A:** The buried remains of an 18th-century Spanish mission. A special machine mounted in an airplane measured minute temperature differences to locate brick and clay in the dirt.

3. **Q:** What did computer executives at IBM facilities in Boca Raton and worldwide, acting on a tip, brace for on May 13, 1988—a Friday the 13th?
**A:** A possible attack by a computer "virus"—a deliberately placed, clandestine program designed like a time bomb to wipe out memory and destroy other programming. It never struck.

4. **Q:** In the late 1970s, the city of Cape Coral, near Fort Myers, built what was then the largest plant in the nation for what method of water purification?
**A:** Reverse osmosis, a process that removes impurities from brackish water.

5. **Q:** A research center for what alternative energy source is near Port Canaveral?
**A:** The 10-acre Florida Solar Energy Center, created by the state legislature in 1974.

6. **Q:** The state's coldest day on record was February 13, 1899, in Tallahassee. How cold did it get?
**A:** Meteorologists recorded a very un-Floridian two degrees below zero!

67

7.  **Q:** The state's hottest day on record was June 29, 1931, in Monticello. How hot did it get?
    **A:** A toasty 109.

8.  **Q:** Key West claims to be the only city in the continental United States to never have experienced what?
    **A:** Frost.

9.  **Q:** What weather event occurred in Miami on January 19, 1977, that people swore would never happen?
    **A:** It snowed.

10. **Q:** What's the largest snowfall amount recorded in Florida?
    **A:** Four inches on February 13, 1899, in Union County.

11. **Q:** Florida has more of what weather phenomenon than any other place in the Northern Hemisphere?
    **A:** Thunderstorms. Only in some areas of the Southern Hemisphere, particularly parts of southern Africa, are there more.

12. **Q:** What weather phenomenon kills more people in Florida than anywhere else in the country?
    **A:** Lightning kills about a half-dozen people and injures another 30 each year.

13. **Q:** What fraction of South Florida's rain falls from mid-May to mid-November?
    **A:** The six-month period—the traditional rainy season—drops 70 percent of the year's rain.

14. **Q:** Who gets more rain in a year: Miami or Seattle?
    **A:** Despite—or, actually, due to—its famous drizzle, the Seattle area

A lightning bolt strikes near the space shuttle launch pad on August 20, 1983. The shuttle launched safely a few hours later. (NASA)

gets only about 38 inches of rain a year. South Florida, drenched by summer thunderstorms, averages 60 inches a year.

15. **Q:** How much rain fell on September 5-6, 1950, in Yankeetown, near Cedar Key?
    **A:** More than three feet! The 38.7-inch rainfall set a national record for a 24-hour period; the record stood for nearly three decades.

## HURRICANES: THE DEADLY WIND

**16. Q:** What can account for as much as 30 percent of the September rainfall in parts of North Florida?
**A:** Hurricanes.

**17. Q:** What boom town was all but destroyed by the September 18, 1926, hurricane?
**A:** Miami.

**18. Q:** What happened "The Night 2,000 Died"?
**A:** A hurricane in and around Lake Okeechobee on September 16, 1928, crumbled a 5-foot dike and sent water rushing out. It was the third-largest single loss of life in American history; estimates of those drowned range from 1,800 to 3,000, but the official death toll of 1,836 prompted the colloquial term for Florida's deadliest night—the night 2,000 died.

**19. Q:** On September 2, 1935, the Labor Day Hurricane, one of the nation's deadliest storms, killed 409 people. Many of them were in the Keys doing what?
**A:** About 256 of the victims were among the 683 World War I veterans who were working in Keys road camps. A Federal Emergency Relief Administration program employed the embittered veterans, who had complained the country forgot them after the war.

**20. Q:** What event surprised meteorologists by bringing only 0.35 inches of rain on Miami in 1941?
**A:** While hurricanes can drop

The 1926 hurricane pulverized booming Miami.(*Miami News*)

several inches of rain in a relatively short period, causing widespread flooding and tidal surges, an October 1941 storm that struck Miami with winds of 123 m.p.h. dropped only 0.35 inches.

**21. Q:** In what city is the National Hurricane Center?
**A:** In 1995, it moved from Coral Gables to Florida International University in western Dade County.

**22. Q:** Under pressure from feminists, what practice did hurricane forecasters discontinue in 1978?
**A:** Naming all hurricanes after women. The practice is believed to date back to World War II servicemen, who named Pacific storms after their wives or girlfriends. Weather officials did it informally as far back as 1941, then officially in 1953. Starting in 1979, every other storm was named for a male.

23. **Q:** What caused plaster to fall, windows to rattle, and items to fly off shelves for about 10 minutes in St. Augustine and Daytona Beach on January 12, 1879?
**A:** An earthquake felt in a 25,000-square-mile area stretching northward to Savannah, Ga.

24. **Q:** What happens a lot in Southern California but almost never in Florida?
**A:** Earthquakes. Seven have been recorded, all minor and all in North Florida. Scientists say there may have been another 30 to 40 since the 1870s. The state's protection comes from the soft limestone base under the peninsula. It acts as a shock absorber for underground shifting.

25. **Q:** What caused a column of smoke and a red glare visible for years in the impenetrable Wakulla swamp west of Tallahassee to disappear in August 1886?
**A:** An earthquake centered near Charleston, S.C. At the time, geologists reported they believed escaping natural gas was ignited by lightning, and the earthquake sealed the fissure, extinguishing the blaze.

26. **Q:** What's bigger: Lake Okeechobee or Rhode Island?
**A:** At some 700 square miles, the second largest freshwater lake wholly within the continental United States is two-thirds the size of Rhode Island.

27. **Q:** What does the St. Johns River do that only a handful of rivers do?

**A:** It flows away from the equator—in this case north, about 276 miles from Lake Helen Blazes in Brevard County to the Atlantic Ocean east of downtown Jacksonville.

28. **Q:** What historical distinction does the Ocala National Forest claim?
**A:** It was the Southeast's first national forest, founded on November 24, 1908.

29. **Q:** What does Paynes Prairie, just south of Gainesville, do about four times every century?
**A:** It turns into Paynes Lake, when natural drains into underground aquifers become clogged.

30. **Q:** What natural feature in North Florida's Alachua County is called the Devil's Millhopper?
**A:** A giant sinkhole.

31. **Q:** What sprawling swamp straddles the Florida-Georgia state line northwest of Jacksonville?
**A:** The Okefenokee Swamp.

32. **Q:** What swamp covers an area of South Florida bigger than Delaware?
**A:** The Big Cypress Swamp covers 2,400 square miles. About 40 percent of the swamp is the Big Cypress National Preserve.

A dredge helps build the giant dike around Lake Okeechobee in the 1960s.

President Harry Truman meets with Seminoles as he dedicates Everglades National Park on December 6, 1947. (Acme Photo)

36. **Q:** What happened in 1973 to a 40-foot natural limestone bridge spanning Miami's Arch Creek? **A:** It fell in.

37. **Q:** During the Ice Age, how far west of its present location was the shoreline of Florida's Gulf Coast? **A:** About 80 miles. The oceans were lower then because much of their water was frozen in glaciers.

38. **Q:** What moves at about three knots just off the Florida coast? **A:** The Gulf Stream.

33. **Q:** What is the "River of Grass" that is the subject of environmentalist Marjory Stoneman Douglas' landmark book? **A:** The Everglades.

34. **Q:** What park did President Harry Truman dedicate on December 6, 1947? **A:** Everglades National Park.

35. **Q:** What underwater formation will you find in the Panhandle's Wakulla County that is believed to be the largest of its kind in the United States? **A:** A system of underwater caves.

# 12
## History:
## Age of Exploration
### (to 1776)

1. **Q:** When Juan Ponce de León waded ashore on Florida's central east coast and declared the North American continent for Spain, on what type of land mass did he believe he had landed?
   **A:** A giant island.

2. **Q:** True or false: Juan Ponce de León named his discovery Florida because he saw many flowers.
   **A:** False. He landed near Easter Sunday, and named the area for Spain's Easter time "Feast of Flowers"—in Spanish, *Pascua Florida.*

3. **Q:** Juan Ponce de León wasn't really looking for the Fountain of Youth, was he?
   **A:** Historians are now convinced the old tale is just that, and that the explorer was looking for silver and gold and new lands and people to conquer for the Spanish.

4. **Q:** What explorer was fatally wounded while battling Indians in the Charlotte Harbor area.
   **A:** Juan Ponce de León was wounded there in 1521 and died later in Havana.

5. **Q:** Who led the first major European expedition into North America's interior in 1539?
   **A:** Hernando de Soto. He is believed to have come ashore at the mouth of Tampa Bay near Bradenton—some historians argue he embarked from Charlotte Harbor or Fort Myers—and later encountered the Mississippi River. He died in 1542 in what is now Arkansas.

An 1855 engraving of Hernando de Soto's landing in Florida in 1539.

6.  **Q:** What holiday was believed celebrated for the first time in the "New World" in 1539?
    **A:** Hernando de Soto, on his trek across the North American continent, spent the winter of 1539-40 in North Florida and is believed to have conducted the first Christmas services in the "New World."

7.  **Q:** What part of the North American continent was once called Florida?
    **A:** All of it, or at least as much as the Spaniards knew existed when they claimed it in the 1500s.

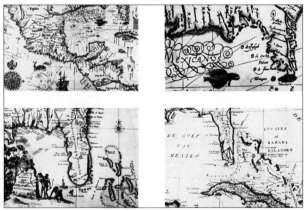

8.  **Q:** What legend did Juan Ortiz's rescue at the hands of an Indian maiden predate by several years?
    **A:** Long before the Pocahontas legend, Ortiz—a Spanish sailor captured by Calusa natives near present-day Tampa—was condemned to death by the chief but spared at the pleading of his eldest daughter. The story made its way back to Spain, where a historian attributed it to British settler Capt. John Smith, although Pocahontas would have been four at the time.

9.  **Q:** How many descendants of the original Indians present when Europeans first came to Florida survive today?
    **A:** None. The original groups, numbering anywhere from 100,000 to 500,000 when explorers first arrived, had all but disappeared within two centuries—massacred, slain in battle with Europeans or each other, sold into slavery or killed by European diseases for which they had no defenses.

10. **Q:** How was Dominican friar Fray Luis Cancer de Barbastro greeted by Calusa natives when he waded ashore in Tampa Bay on June 26, 1549?
    **A:** They clubbed him to death.

These four maps show images of Florida in the 16th and 17th centuries (Historical Museum of Southern Florida)

11. **Q:** Explorers originally called the Tampa Bay area natives "too rough to conquer and too stubborn to" what?
    **A:** Convert.

12. **Q:** The Spanish established more than 60 of what institutions in colonial Florida?
    **A:** Catholic missions.

13. **Q:** Why was the St. Johns River originally called *Rivière de la Mai?*
    **A:** The Jacksonville area was first settled in 1564 by the French, who called the giant waterway "The River of May" because the first French exploration of the area had taken place in May 1562.

**ST. AUGUSTINE: THE FIRST CITY**

14. **Q:** How did Matanzas Inlet, south of St. Augustine, get its name?
    **A:** It's Spanish for "massacre" or "slaughter." Spanish explorers slew 300 French settlers there in 1565, crushing French expansion into Florida. It was the first bloodshed between European colonists on the North American mainland.

15. **Q:** What kind of people were the Huguenots, who first settled in the Jacksonville area in the mid-1500s?
    **A:** They were French Protestants.

16. **Q:** Which came first: St. Augustine or Plymouth Rock?
    **A:** St. Augustine is the nation's oldest continuous city. It was set- tled more than four centuries ago, in 1565. It is 42 years older than the colony at Jamestown, established in 1607, and had been around for 55 years when the Pilgrims landed at Plymouth Rock in 1620.

17. **Q:** Who has owned Florida longer: the United States or Spain?
    **A:** Spain. Florida was under Spanish rule for a total of 236 years: 198 years from 1565 until 1763, when they traded it to England for Cuba, then for another 38 from 1783 until 1821, when they gave it to America. Florida will celebrate 236 years under American rule in the year 2057.

18. **Q:** The first European settlement in Florida wasn't at St. Augustine, but where?

    **A:** Charlotte Harbor. The colony of 200, founded a quarter-century before St. Augustine, lasted for about six months before it fell victim to disease and Indian attacks. Its exact location is unknown.

19. **Q:** Which city almost beat St. Augustine as America's oldest?
    **A:** Pensacola. Don Tristan de Luna and a fleet of 13 ships founded a settlement there in 1559, six years before St. Augustine was established. But a storm sank most of the ships and the colony was abandoned two years later; Pensacola was not resettled for another 125 years.

20. **Q:** What 200-foot stainless-steel religious symbol towering over St. Augustine commemorates the arrival of Europeans in the "New World"?
    **A:** A cross.

21. **Q:** What did England's Sir Francis Drake do at St. Augustine on May 20, 1586?
    **A:** He plundered the town.

22. **Q:** A candlelight procession through the streets of St. Augustine every December and June recreates what colonial tra- dition?
    **A:** Locking the town for the night. As a protection against attack or civil disorder, the gates of the city were locked each night, guards were posted and people were required to carry lights on darkened streets.

## CASTILLO DE SAN MARCOS: AN UNCONQUERED FORTRESS

**23. Q:** St. Augustine's Castillo de San Marcos, one of the oldest man-made structures in the United States, is what kind of structure?
**A:** The awe-inspiring Spanish masonry fortress was built between 1672 and 1695 to protect the city from seaborne invaders.

**24. Q:** The Castillo de San Marcos fortress was made from coquina, which is what kind of substance?
**A:** It's a rock made from sea shells. The walls run from nine to 20 feet thick, and three sides are surrounded by a moat.

**25. Q:** What has no one been able to do to St. Augustine's 300-year-old Castillo de San Marcos?
**A:** Seize it in battle.

**26. Q:** What bay did explorers originally call *Espiritu Santu* (Holy Spirit)?
**A:** Tampa Bay.

**27. Q:** Why did explorers name the islands west of Key West the Dry Tortugas?
**A:** They were called "dry" because they contained no fresh water. Tortugas is the Spanish word for turtles, of which the explorers saw and captured many.

**28. Q:** What did the Spanish originally call *Los Martires*—The Martyrs?
**A:** The Florida Keys. Many ships met their fates on the shallow reefs surrounding the islands.

**29. Q:** Why did Quaker settler Jonathan Dickinson and his family have to walk from the Jupiter area to St. Augustine in 1696?
**A:** They had been shipwrecked.

**30. Q:** Who came first to Florida: Seminoles or Europeans?

**A:** The Seminoles were an offshoot of the Creek tribes of Alabama who migrated down to Florida in the 1700s, long after the Europeans' arrival.

A Seminole woman with a large tool once used to crush corn. (Fort Lauderdale Historical Society).

**31. Q:** Where did the Plate Fleet—about a dozen ships that sank off Fort Pierce in a 1715 storm—get its name?

A: It had an estimated booty of $14 million, much of it in *plata*— Spanish for silver.

32. Q: What have 1,200 to 1,800 ships done off the Florida coast in the last 4-1/2 centuries?
A: They went to the bottom.

33. Q: There were once two Floridas. Where were they?
A: From Spanish colonization until Florida joined the United States in 1821, there were two territories. East Florida covered the peninsula from Tallahassee over and down to Key West. West Florida stretched almost to New Orleans, and included large chunks of southern Alabama, Mississippi, and Louisiana.

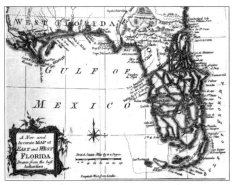

Once, there were two Floridas. The two territories stretched almost to New Orleans.

34. Q: The alleged loss of what part of his anatomy led a British smuggler to talk England into invading the Spanish-held Florida territories in 1740?
A: "The War of Jenkins' Ear" started after smuggler Robert Jenkins told Parliament in 1739 that Spaniards had boarded his boat seven years earlier off the Florida coast and cut off his ear, which he pulled from his pocket to show to the aghast legislators. The British coveted the Floridas and were looking for an excuse. The invasion failed, but England got the territories in 1763 in a land exchange. The "ear" turned out to be fake.

35. Q: What was the social position of most settlers of Rollestown, near Palatka?
A: The 200 British settlers recruited by Denys Rolle in the 1760s included some of London's most notorious vagrants, bums, and debtors. Not being the most stable of people, when times got tough, they abandoned the settlement.

36. Q: What did England trade to Spain in exchange for Florida in 1763?
A: The British had wrested away Havana during the Seven Years' War, fought in North America as the French and Indian War. At the Treaty of Paris, ending the conflict, they ransomed Cuba back to the Spanish for the Floridas.

37. Q: What did nearly every Spaniard in the Floridas do in 1763?
A: They left. In an unprecedented, complete swap of population, the few thousand Spaniards went to Havana, other Spanish territories, or Spain, and were replaced by the British.

# 13
## History:
## Redcoats to Rebellion
### (1776-1861)

1. **Q:** What side did the Florida territories take in the American Revolution?
   **A:** Residents of the 14th and 15th British colonies—recently traded from Spain—had no beef with the king. Americans John Hancock and Samuel Adams were hung in effigy in St. Augustine.

2. **Q:** Why did the population of the Floridas increase from 8,000 to 30,000 during the American Revolution?
   **A:** Because the territories stayed loyal to England, many loyalists, called Tories, fled there.

3. **Q:** Why did many blacks in the Floridas support England during the American Revolution?
   **A:** The British promised slaves freedom in exchange for their loyalty; blacks saw King George as a liberator instead of an oppressor.

4. **Q:** Did the Revolutionary War come to the Floridas?
   **A:** Rebels chased some loyalists and there were four inconclusive skirmishes.

5. **Q:** What happened June 30, 1778, at Alligator Creek, west of Jacksonville?

**A:** One of two major land skirmishes of the Revolutionary War in the Floridas. Three hundred American cavalrymen attacked 450 redcoats near the town of Callahan, and after a brief confrontation, the Americans withdrew with a loss of 13 men. The British lost nine. At an earlier battle, on May 17, 1777, an invading American expedition was attacked by redcoats at nearby Thomas Creek. The Americans retreated with heavy casualties. It and the Alligator Creek battle, while not on a par with Yorktown, were still significant: they halted American advances into the British Floridas.

6. **Q:** During the American Revolution, the British lost West Florida to what other country that had taken advantage of England's vulnerability?
   **A:** Its old nemesis, Spain, seized the capital of Pensacola in 1781, taking control of the territory.

7. **Q:** In 1783, the *East Florida Gazette* became what is believed to have been the first of its kind in Florida. What was it?

77

**A:** A newspaper. Run by a British loyalist in sympathetic St. Augustine, the *Gazette* was more a propaganda sheet than a chronicle of events. Its publisher was true to his journalistic roots, however, when he swallowed his dismay and rushed out an "extra" about the British losing.

8.  **Q:** What do some historians believe took place off the coast of Cape Canaveral some two years after the last battle of the American Revolution?
    **A:** The real last battle of the conflict. On March 10, 1783, a U.S. ship and a French ship taking gold from Havana to Rhode Island were attacked by three British Navy ships, and the ensuing 40-minute battle left two British sailors and eight Americans dead. The ships were able to continue on and deliver their gold.

9.  **Q:** What did the British do with the Floridas after the American Revolution?
    **A:** Deciding they'd had enough of America, they held onto Canada and some Caribbean islands and washed their hands of the rest, conceding independence to the 13 colonies and returning the Floridas to Spain in 1783 in exchange for the Spanish-seized Bahamas.

10. **Q:** What did the East Florida Patriots declare in St. Augustine in 1812?
    **A:** They seized the territory from Spain and declared "The Republic of East Florida" with plans to later "surrender" to the United States, which had put them up to it. Spain protested and President James Madison said he'd never heard of the "Patriots." Alone, they lasted a few months.

11. **Q:** The flag of the Republic of East Florida showed a silhouette of a soldier and bayonet and the words *Salus populi lex suprema.* What did that mean?
    **A:** "The safety of the people, the supreme law."

12. **Q:** Was Florida ever its own country?
    **A:** Yes; twice. Once during the Patriots' Rebellion of the 19th century—actually, just East Florida—then in the days after the state seceded and before it joined the Confederacy.

13. **Q:** The quiet village of Fernandina Beach at the northeast corner of Florida says it has been under how many different flags?
    **A:** Eight. In order: The flags of France, Spain, England, and the Republic of East Florida; the "Green Cross of Florida"; and the flags of Mexico, the Confederacy, and the United States. The Green Cross and Mexico flags were flown by mercenaries who briefly seized the town.

14. **Q:** What small North Florida town was so filled with pirates, thieves, and smugglers that President James Monroe called it "a festering fleshpot"?
    **A:** Fernandina Beach.

15. **Q:** In the 1800s, Apalachicola was the nation's third largest port for what commodity?
    **A:** Cotton. It shipped $6 million to $8 million a year from southern plantations.

16. **Q:** In 1816, American troops were sent to destroy "Negro Fort," an abandoned British fort in the Panhandle that had been occupied by more than 300 escaped slaves. How long did it take?

**A:** The fifth shot hit the ammunition pile. All but 30 died instantly.

17. **Q:** How long did mercenary Sir General Gregor MacGregor rule Fernandina Beach in 1817?
    **A:** About two months. MacGregor—the origin and legitimacy of his self-professed monikers are unknown—claimed he had five boats and a thousand men, but he really had only 150 men. His plan was to take northeast Florida from Spain and turn it over to the United States. When U.S. aid did not come, he slunk off.

18. **Q:** What did America pay Spain for the Floridas in 1819?
    **A:** Five million dollars. Actually, no money changed hands; the U.S. government simply agreed to take over damage claims to American property owners in the Floridas. In 1821, Florida took possession of the territories, reduced their borders and created a single Florida territory.

19. **Q:** What large piece of property in the Florida Keys did Juan P. Salas sell to John W. Simonton for $2,000 on December 20, 1821?
    **A:** Key West. Salas, who had received the island as a Spanish grant in 1815, sold it to American businessman Simonton in Havana. Simonton took possession on January 19, 1822, thus establishing South Florida's first permanent community.

20. **Q:** A special fleet was organized by the U.S. Navy in Key West in 1822 to battle what outlaws?
    **A:** Pirates. The West Indian Squadron had 17 ships and 1,100 men and nabbed 79 of the estimated 2,000 pirates plying the seas.

21. **Q:** What did three log cabins house in Tallahassee in 1824?
    **A:** The territorial government offices.

22. **Q:** What Revolutionary War hero was given $200,000 and 24,000 acres of land near Tallahassee by Congress on August 15, 1824?
    **A:** The French patriot Marquis de Lafayette, crucial in helping American colonists obtain independence. He had been financially ruined in the Reign of Terror that followed the revolution in his homeland. He never got to Florida to see his land.

23. **Q:** The nephew of what world emperor lived in Tallahassee?
    **A:** Achille Murat, nephew of Napoleon, moved to Tallahassee in 1825. He was an attorney, a judge, and a bank executive.

24. **Q:** What cities did Florida's first federally-funded road, built in 1826, connect?
    **A:** The past and present capitals of St. Augustine and Tallahassee.

25. **Q:** The first owner of what is now the Audubon House in Key West stocked it with furniture from what source?
    **A:** Shipwrecks. The owner, a wrecker, hosted famed naturalist John James Audubon in 1832 and the building became the Audubon House museum in 1960.

26. **Q:** What happened on December 28, 1835, moments after Major Francis Dade told his troops "Have a glad heart; our difficulties and dangers are over now . . . "?
    **A:** He and his company of more than 100 soldiers were massacred by Seminoles, helping to spark the Second Seminole War and earning Dade the distinction of having Florida's most well-known county named for him.

27. **Q:** What modern fraternity prank did Seminoles approximate in 1836 to goad soldiers at Fort Cooper into wasting their ammunition?
**A:** They "mooned" the troops, hoping this insult would infuriate the men into shooting at them and using up all their bullets.

28. **Q:** When U.S. soldiers abandoned Fort Alabama on April 26, 1836, what did they leave behind for the Seminoles?
**A:** A booby-trap. They placed a rifle with its barrel in a bag of gunpowder and rigged its trigger to the door of the powder magazine. They had gone less than two miles from the fort when they heard a blast. They later learned three Indians had died in the explosion. The fort was later re-established and named Fort Foster. It is now a historic site northeast of Tampa.

29. **Q:** On July 23, 1836, as he roasted in a fire lit by Seminoles at the base of the Cape Florida lighthouse on Key Biscayne, the keeper, trapped at the top, decided to light a cache of dynamite, which would kill him instantly instead of slowly. What happened?
**A:** The explosion extinguished the fire. The keeper survived.

30. **Q:** What was ironic about the death of U.S. Army Major David Moniac at the hands of Seminole Indians at the Battle of Wahoo Swamp, on November 21, 1836?
**A:** Moniac was himself an Indian—a member of the Creek tribe, of which the Seminoles are an offshoot.

31. **Q:** What flag were U.S. soldiers carrying when they captured Seminole warrior Osceola and 70 of his warriors near St. Augustine on October 21, 1837?
**A:** A white flag of truce. The trick outraged the country and helped build sympathy toward the Seminoles. Osceola died in captivity in January 1838 at Fort Moultrie, S.C. Two decades after the Seminoles' shameful capture, the general who had ordered it was still defending himself.

The great Seminole warrior Osceola.

An explosion actually saved the Cape Florida lighthouse in 1836. It's still standing. (Miami-Metro Department of Publicity and Tourism)

**32. Q:** Where did the town of Christmas, east of Orlando, get its name?
**A:** It is the site of a fort built during the Second Seminole War; construction began on December 25, 1837. The fort was later abandoned, but a nearby museum displays a reconstruction.

**33. Q:** Near what south-central Florida town did the decisive battle of the Second Seminole War take place?
**A:** Okeechobee. Gen. Zachary Taylor, later to become president, led troops against Seminoles on Christmas Day 1837. The Seminoles were eventually chased into the swamps or captured and sent to Oklahoma.

Gen. Zachary Taylor in the field. (Acme Photo)

**34. Q:** After the battle of Okeechobee in 1837, during the Second Seminole War, Gen. Zachary Taylor accused a group of Missouri volunteers under his command of what?
**A:** Cowardice. The volunteers were later cleared.

**35. Q:** What fraction of the 10,169 American soldiers serving in the Second Seminole War who died were killed by disease rather than in battle?
**A:** Three of four—1,072 of the 1,400 who died—fell to disease, only 328 in battle.

**36. Q:** What happened to the town where Florida's constitution was written in 1838?
**A:** St. Joseph, in the Panhandle, disappeared—victim of a yellow fever epidemic and two hurricanes. Nearby Port St. Joe is its only reminder.

**37. Q:** What happened to the family of Henry Perrine on Indian Key on August 7, 1840?
**A:** Seminoles attacked them, massacring the botanist and six others on the tiny key. His family escaped.

**38. Q:** What was unusual about the group dressed in Shakespearian theatrical garb that gathered in front of a fort in 1841?
**A:** They were Seminoles. The group, led by Coacoochee (Wildcat), had seized the costumes the year before in an attack on a traveling theater troupe near St. Augustine in which four men died.

**39. Q:** What happened to abolitionist Jonathan Walker in November 1844?
**A:** Convicted of trying to help slaves escape, his hand was branded with the letters "SS" for "slave stealer." The incident flamed anti-South sentiment.

40. **Q:** When Florida was being considered for statehood, a U.S. senator from Virginia called it "a land of swamps, of quagmires, of frogs and alligators, and mosquitoes" and said no one would want to emigrate there even from what place?
**A:** Hell.

41. **Q:** How did Florida's status change on March 3, 1845?
**A:** It became the 27th state.

42. **Q:** What midwestern state was established along with Florida?
**A:** Iowa. Congress then was in the practice of admitting northern and southern states in pairs.

43. **Q:** What state building advertised some of its offices for renters in the *Tallahassee Floridian* on January 15, 1848?
**A:** When the state capitol building opened, the government was so small it couldn't fill the place and some offices were rented out to private businesses.

44. **Q:** The East Florida Seminary opened January 3, 1853, in Ocala. Its three wooden buildings had been a private academy. None of the first students were more than 14 years old. What did it eventually become?
**A:** The University of Florida.

45. **Q:** The Third Seminole War began when chief Billy Bowlegs refused to do something many of his fellow Seminoles had already done. What?
**A:** Bowlegs would not move west from Florida, despite an 1853 state law forbidding Indians to reside in the state. A three-year conflict ended when Bowlegs and 165 Seminoles were promised financial aid and left peacefully for Oklahoma.

46. **Q:** What was the historic significance of the Third Seminole War, a three-year conflict that ended in 1856?
**A:** It was the last Indian uprising east of the Mississippi River.

# 14

## History:
## Civil War in Florida

### (1861-1865)

1. **Q:** What side did Florida take in the Civil War?
   **A:** The Confederacy.

2. **Q:** How many Floridians voted for Abraham Lincoln in 1860?
   **A:** Not a one, state records claim.

Abraham Lincoln was not popular in secessionist Florida.

3. **Q:** What action by Florida on January 11, 1861, prompted former Gov. Richard Keith Call, who had supported the Union, to say "You have opened the gates of hell"?
   **A:** Secession.

4. **Q:** What action by Florida in 1861 did the Panhandle's Walton and Liberty Counties oppose?
   **A:** Secession.

5. **Q:** Was Florida one of the first or last states to leave the Union just before the Civil War?
   **A:** It was third, after South Carolina and Mississippi.

6. **Q:** What was the historic significance of the railroad between Fernandina Beach and Cedar Key, which began operating on March 1, 1861?
   **A:** The Florida Railroad Company, founded by Florida U.S. senator David Yulee, also known as David Levy, was Florida's first cross-state railroad. Its strategic importance made it a target, and much of it was destroyed during the Civil War. Terminals at both ends were burned, and retreating Confederates tore up some of the tracks.

7. **Q:** What did Florida do on April 22, 1861?
   **A:** The state, which had technically been an independent nation since it seceded from the Union on January 11, joined the Confederacy.

8. **Q:** What cabinet position did Floridian Stephen R. Mallory hold in the Confederate cabinet?

A: Mallory, a resident of Key West and Florida U.S. senator from 1851 to 1861, was Confederate Secretary of the Navy. He pioneered development of submarines and iron-clad ships.

9. Q: At the time of the Civil War, Florida had 60,000 of what?
A: Slaves.

10. Q: During the Civil War, the Jupiter Lighthouse was seized by Confederates who stole something and hid it. What did they take?
A: The lighting equipment, so Confederate merchant ships could get past the Union blockade. After the war, the mechanism was recovered and returned to use.

## FLORIDA FEEDS THE CONFEDERACY

11. Q: From 1861 to 1863, what did Jake Summerlin sell the Confederacy 35,000 of for $8 each?
A: Cows. Summerlin, the king of Florida cattle, once reigned over an empire that stretched from Fort Meade, in Central Florida, down to Fort Myers.

12. Q: For what food was Florida the primary source in the later part of the Civil War?
A: Beef. When Texas was cut off from the Confederacy, Florida became the rebels' main supplier.

13. Q: What did the rebels' "Cow Cavalry" do during the Civil War?
A: For much of the war, Florida was the Confederacy's major beef supplier, and the "cavalry" was organized to stop the Union's practice of killing cattle in the field to keep fresh beef out of soldiers' bellies.

14. Q: What important food item did the small town of Cedar Key help provide the Confederacy during the Civil War?
A: Salt. It was made by boiling ocean water in large basins.

15. Q: Where did Florida operate a soldiers' hospital during the Civil War?
A: In Richmond, Va. During the war, each Confederate state operated a hospital near the front for its own soldiers. The building is now a furniture warehouse.

16. Q: Why did Fort Clinch, just north of Fernandina Beach on the very tip of the state, play little or no role in the Civil War?
A: Work on the garrison began some 15 years before the Civil War, but it was never finished.

Fort Clinch is now a state park. (Florida News Bureau)

Union and rebel troops took turns occupying it; now it is a state park and guides dressed in period garb recreate the past.

17. Q: What Civil War general had been stationed at Fort Pierce in 1841, during the Second Seminole War?

A: William Tecumseh Sherman, who would later burn Atlanta. He was fresh out of West Point and was assigned to duty as a second lieutenant.

18. **Q:** What future Confederate general was stationed at Polk County's Fort Meade before the Civil War?

    **A:** Lt. Gen. Thomas J. "Stonewall" Jackson served as a first lieutenant at the Central Florida fort before becoming one of America's leading military figures and perhaps the most famous ever accidentally killed by his own men. On May 2, 1863, while scouting ahead at night in Virginia, he was mistaken for an enemy soldier and shot. He died of pneumonia 10 days later.

19. **Q:** When 5,000 Union troops squared off with about 5,000 rebels on Feb. 20, 1864, in the small North Florida town of Olustee, who won?

    **A:** The largest battle on Florida soil left 203 Union troops and 93 Confederates dead. The Union loss ended hopes of reclaiming Florida before the end of the war.

20. **Q:** With most able-bodied soldiers off at the war front, who helped saved Tallahassee from Union invaders at the Battle of Natural Bridge in 1865?

    **A:** Old men and wounded soldiers and military school cadets, some as young as 14, from the West Florida Seminary—now Florida State University.

21. **Q:** The Battle of Natural Bridge, in 1865, preserved Tallahassee as the only Confederate state capital east of the Mississippi River with what distinction?

A: It was the only one never to fall during the war.

22. **Q:** What Florida city was never part of the Confederacy?

    **A:** Key West, then isolated from the mainland and a major federal military city, never left Union control.

23. **Q:** Why did Confederate Secretary of State Judah Benjamin come to Florida in the final days of the Civil War in 1865?

    **A:** To escape to the Bahamas. He hid in the Gamble mansion in Ellenton, near Bradenton, now a museum.

The Gamble mansion, near Bradenton, is now a museum.

24. **Q:** What did Florida's governor do in the last days of the Civil War?

    **A:** Governor John Milton—a descendant of the family of the famed poet—was devastated by the Confederacy's defeat and the prospect of Union occupation. He died of a bullet to the head at his Panhandle plantation, an apparent suicide victim. In his last message to the state legislature, he had said, "Death would be preferable to reunion."

25. **Q:** What did Maryland doctor Samuel Mudd do in 1865 that got him sentenced to life at the prison at Fort Jefferson, west of Key West?

**A:** He unknowingly set the broken leg of John Wilkes Booth, assassin of President Abraham Lincoln, and was wrongly convicted of conspiracy in Lincoln's death. When the barren island fort in the Dry Tortugas was struck by yellow fever, Mudd was freed in order to save lives. He was later reprieved, but grandson Richard D. Mudd spent his life unsuccessfully lobbying presidents to overturn the conviction.

26. **Q:** In terms of economic devastation, where did Florida rank among rebel states in the Civil War?
    **A:** Of all Confederate states, only Virginia suffered more.

27. **Q:** What author whose book helped lead to the Civil War wintered in Jacksonville's Mandarin community from 1867 to 1884?
    **A:** Harriet Beecher Stowe. Her 1851 *Uncle Tom's Cabin* and its portrayal of slave life in the South further polarized Americans on the issue and helped speed the slide toward civil war. In Florida, Stowe grew and shipped citrus and wrote a book, *Palmetto Leaves*, describing the area.

28. **Q:** What holiday do Florida and only a few other states celebrate on April 26?
    **A:** Confederate Memorial Day.

29. **Q:** What's unusual about the Civil War monument in Lynn Haven, near Panama City?
    **A:** It is one of the few in the former Confederacy that honor Union soldiers. It was erected in 1920 by a Yankee veterans' colony.

30. **Q:** What military items were thrown into Lake Desoto, in Lake City, just after the Civil War and not found until 1982?
    **A:** Rifles. Union occupation troops had left their weapons outside while they ate in a restaurant. While cleaning the lake in 1982, salvagers found 16 Springfield rifles, apparently tossed in while the soldiers ate. Some are now on display at the city's public library.

31. **Q:** Where in Florida did searchers recently find 800,000 pounds of personal items from Civil War soldiers?
    **A:** In the *Maple Leaf*, a Union ship hit by a rebel mine and sunk in the St. Johns River in Jacksonville. Mud kept the items in a vacuum and left them remarkably preserved, making this perhaps the country's largest collection of preserved Civil War items.

# 15
## History:
## The Boom Years
### (1865-1941)

1. **Q:** What did a majority of Panhandle voters opt for in 1869?
   **A:** They voted to become part of Alabama. But that state, financially devastated by the Civil War, couldn't come up with $1 million Florida wanted for roads and other public works. So the area stayed in Florida.

2. **Q:** What did the Spanish government in Cuba do to 53 people, including eight Americans, in 1873, sparking an international incident?
   **A:** The 53, who had tried to smuggle guns aboard the ship *Virginius* to aid Cuban rebels, were executed.

Gilbert's Bar House of Refuge, Hutchinson Island. (Florida News Bureau)

3. **Q:** For whom was the Gilbert's Bar House of Refuge north of Stuart built in 1875?
   **A:** It was a refuge for people shipwrecked off Florida's coast. The building is the only one of nine houses built along the coast that still stands. It's now a museum.

4. **Q:** What cargo did the *Providencia* spill when it wrecked on what is now Palm Beach?
   **A:** The ship, loaded with 20,000 coconuts bound from Trinidad to Spain, ran aground January 9, 1878. Residents bought the coconuts at the salvage price of 2-1/2 cents each and planted them. Within a decade, the area was filled with palm trees, inspiring the name Palm Beach.

5. **Q:** Why was West Palm Beach originally established?
   **A:** As a railroad depot for the wealthy part-time and permanent residents of Palm Beach and as a place for their workers and servants to live.

6. **Q:** How much did wealthy Philadelphian Hamilton Disston pay per acre to buy four million acres of Central Florida in 1881?

Early West Palm Beach, with Palm Beach across the lake. (Historical Society of Palm Beach County)

Hamilton Disston, one of Florida's first entrepreneurs

**A:** He paid a cool million dollars—25 cents an acre.

7.  **Q:** What did the Internal Improvement Act allow the state to offer for tiny amounts or free in the second half of the 19th century?
    **A:** Land. Florida wanted to encourage development and growth.

8.  **Q:** What famous Indian leader was imprisoned at Fort Pickens, near Pensacola?
    **A:** Geronimo and about 50 other Apaches were kept in the prison from 1886 to 1888.

9.  **Q:** The need for what public institution sparked the birth of Lee County?
    **A:** A schoolhouse. When Fort Myers' only schoolhouse burned down in 1886, Monroe County, with its seat in Key West, refused to pay for a new one. The Fort Myers area then demanded its own county, and Lee was split off from Monroe by an act of the state legislature on May 2, 1887.

10. **Q:** Eatonville, a town of 3,000 in suburban Orlando that celebrated its centennial in 1987, is the oldest city in America founded strictly by and for what ethnic group?
    **A:** Blacks.

11. **Q:** What did the American Medical Society do in 1885 that sparked the influx of elderly to the St. Petersburg area?
    **A:** The group declared the Pinellas peninsula to have the best climate in America.

12. **Q:** What foreign city had a town in Tampa Bay named for it, then changed its name, then changed it back?
    **A:** St. Petersburg, Russia. Peter Demens founded the Florida city in 1888 and named it for his Russian hometown, which was renamed Leningrad after the Soviet revolution and reverted to St. Petersburg when the Soviet Union collapsed at the end of 1991.

13. **Q:** What did a group of farmers, cowboys, and businessmen do in Manatee County in the 1880s after deciding local law and order was insufficient?
    **A:** They formed the Sara Sota Vigilantes. Originally designed to keep out carpetbaggers and new

settlers, the group of about 20 people punished and sometimes killed those on whom they thought the law had been too lenient. In a spectacular trial in nearby Arcadia that was covered by newsmen from across America, three were convicted. One served three years; the other two escaped jail. But their group had been broken.

14. **Q:** What did an angry mob do to outlaws Mike Kelly and Jim Champion on February 18, 1891?
**A:** The two murder and robbery suspects were pulled from a Gainesville jail and lynched.

15. **Q:** After "Commodore" Ralph Middleton Munroe built his home, the Barnacle, on Miami's Biscayne Bay in 1891, the widower remarried, but the home's design prohibited expanding up or out. What did he do?
**A:** He jacked up the entire home and built another floor below it.

Ralph Middleton Munroe jacked up his Coconut Grove home, the Barnacle, to add a floor.

16. **Q:** For what purpose was the Moorish-influenced, minaret-topped Tampa University built?
**A:** Developer Henry Plant built the Tampa Bay hotel in 1891 for the then-outrageous cost of $3 million. The downtown landmark was sold to the city in 1905 and became the college's main building in 1933.

## REVOLUTION AND WAR TO OUR SOUTH

17. **Q:** Which famous Cuban revolutionary made his New Pines speech on November 27, 1891, in a Tampa cigar factory?
**A:** José Martí, then only 38, electrified the cigarmakers in Tampa's predominantly Cuban Ybor City district, calling on Cubans to rise like *piños nuevos*—new pines—and drive Spanish colonialism from their beloved homeland. The speech helped drum up support for the effort to oust Spain. Martí died in battle May 19, 1895.

18. **Q:** An attempt to invade what country began from Florida January 10, 1895?

**A:** Revolutionary José Martí and others had loaded three boats for an incursion into Cuba to oust colonial Spain. The boats were seized by U.S. officials, who feared allowing a revolt against a friendly nation to start on their soil.

19. **Q:** What famous military squadron, commanded by a future president, assembled in Tampa for war at the end of the 19th century?
**A:** Teddy Roosevelt's Rough Riders prepared to embark for Cuba and fight the Spanish-American War.

Teddy Roosevelt prepared for war in Tampa.

**20. Q:** What ship left the Florida Keys on January 24, 1898, on its final voyage, which ended with America at war?

**A:** The *Maine* left Florida for Havana, where it was blown up and sunk on February 15, killing 260 and leading to the Spanish-American War.

**21. Q:** How long was Miami's Fort Brickell in operation?
**A:** Less than a year. The "fort," built in 1898 during the Spanish-American War amid fears of Spanish invasion from Cuba, consisted of an earth mound, a magazine and two guns. By the end of the year the guns had been removed.

**22. Q:** Henry Flagler's 1,500-guest Royal Poinciana Hotel on Palm Beach was reportedly so big that bellhops used what unusual mode of transportation to deliver messages?
**A:** They reportedly rode bicycles down the hallways of the hotel, opened in February 1894 as the world's largest wooden hotel.

**23. Q:** What famous artist painted Florida cowboys during a visit in 1895?
**A:** Frederic Remington.

**24. Q:** According to an 1896-1897 guide to South Florida, what was the daily off-season rate at one hotel on Palm Beach?
**A:** The Dellmore Cottage would cost you $2.50 a day.

**25. Q:** Historians believe Julia Tuttle sent Henry Flagler something in 1895 that changed South Florida history. What did she send?
**A:** Flagler intended to go no further south than Palm Beach, but

after a freeze devastated North Florida, the "mother of Miami" reportedly sent him flowers to encourage him to come to frost-free Miami.

**26. Q:** What transaction on October 24, 1895, was called "Miami's birth certificate?"
**A:** Henry Flagler and Julia Tuttle signed a deal to continue Flagler's railroad to Miami. The deal gave Flagler half of Tuttle's land, much of it now in downtown Miami.

**27. Q:** What route did the famed "barefoot mailmen" follow to complete their appointed rounds?
**A:** The postal employees shed their shoes and walked the beach between Miami and the Palm Beach area at the ocean's edge, where the sand is wet and firm.

**28. Q:** What fate befell barefoot mailman James E. Hamilton while crossing Hillsboro Inlet near Pompano Beach with his mail?
**A:** Some belongings were found at

one end of the inlet; his body was never found. Fellow pioneers speculated he drowned or was killed by a shark or an alligator.

29. **Q:** When the Dade County seat was moved from Juno Beach to Miami in 1899, what parts of the city's jail were shipped by barge with their contents still inside?
**A:** The cells were loaded on barges with the prisoners still in them.

30. **Q:** What major Florida city was nearly destroyed by a fire on May 3, 1901?
**A:** Jacksonville. The blaze destroyed 2,400 buildings and 466 acres, drove 10,000 people from their homes and killed seven.

### FLORIDA'S FIRST UNIVERSITY

31. **Q:** What did Florida residents pay in tuition when the University of Florida opened in 1906?
**A:** Nothing. Out-of-state students paid $20.

32. **Q:** What was dormitory rent when the University of Florida opened in 1906?
**A:** $2.50 a month.

33. **Q:** When the state decided to place the University of Florida in Gainesville, what had been the second choice?
**A:** Lake City.

34. **Q:** What would a proposed ordinance have regulated in the skies over Kissimmee in 1908?
**A:** Air traffic. Airplanes and other machines flying 10 feet to 20 miles over the cow town had to buy licenses or face a $500 fine or 90

days "in the calaboose." It would also be illegal to drop anything from the air or collide with a telephone pole or public building. The ordinance never passed.

35. **Q:** In 1909, a convoy of vehicles traveled from Tampa to Jacksonville to show the need for roads. How long did the trip take?
**A:** You can now make the 200-mile trip completely by interstate highway—I-4 to I-95—in about 3-1/2 hours. The 1909 group's round trip took four days.

36. **Q:** How did pioneer Henry Flagler travel to Key West on January 12, 1912, for the first time ever?
**A:** The ailing Flagler, a year away from death, rode the first train into Key West, inaugurating the extension of the railroad to the southernmost city. About 15,000 residents came out to watch the five cars arrive at 9:43 a.m.

37. **Q:** How long did the railroad to Key West operate?
**A:** Only 23 years; the 1935 Labor Day hurricane wiped it out, and its remains were replaced by the Overseas Highway in 1938.

Despite the gallant efforts of its builders, the railroad to Key West lasted only two decades. (Historical Museum of Southern Florida)

38. **Q:** Until 1912, what physical phenomenon could you see on the Miami River northwest of downtown Miami?
**A:** A waterfall. The 6-foot drop and rapids disappeared when canals were built to reroute the river's course to Biscayne Bay.

39. **Q:** Of what material was the first bridge to Miami Beach constructed?
**A:** Wood. The 2-1/2 mile Collins Bridge, opened on June 12, 1913, then claimed to be the world's longest wooden bridge.

The Collins Bridge, built in 1913, was replaced in 1925 by the Venetian Causeway. (Miami-Metro News Bureau)

40. **Q:** What did George Merrick, founder of Coral Gables, name the town after?
**A:** His family home, built in 1906 of native limestone rock.

41. **Q:** A 2-1/2 hour flight from Key West on May 17, 1913, was the first ever from Florida to what foreign capital?
**A:** Havana.

42. **Q:** On October 14, 1913, Florida U.S. Rep. Frank Clark wrote the state's governor, suggesting immigrants from what country be banned from Florida?
**A:** Japan.

43. **Q:** According to a 1913 newspaper advertisement, what was the rate at the Hotel Cromanton near Panama City?
**A:** Rooms were $1.50 a day, $7 a week with meals.

44. **Q:** For what kind of vehicle was the nation's first training school opened on December 1, 1914, in Pensacola?
**A:** It was the first air training school.

45. **Q:** Why did the U.S. government seize the assets of a Panhandle lumber company during World War I?
**A:** The foreign-owned German-American Lumber Company was seized in 1917, as America warred with Germany in World War I.

46. **Q:** During World War I, valuable minerals to aid the war effort were found in a settlement south of Jacksonville, and a company bought the settlement, naming it Mineral City. After the war, the operation closed down and the city got its current name, which means "old bridge" and stems from a town in Spain. Name the town.
**A:** Ponte Vedra Beach.

47. **Q:** Just after World War I, a nationwide shortage of a crop left it available only in Hastings, near Palatka. Buyers poured in and the militia had to be called to protect bulging local banks. Name the crop
**A:** Potatoes.

48. **Q:** In the fall of 1918, 30,000 people in Jacksonville got something, and by the time the crisis had passed, more than 460 were dead. What did they get?
    **A:** The flu.

49. **Q:** When President Warren G. Harding vacationed at the Flamingo Hotel in Miami Beach in 1921, who—or what—was his golf caddy?
    **A:** In a publicity scheme dreamed up by hotel owner Carl Fisher, Harding's caddy was Carl II— Fisher's baby elephant.

50. **Q:** How much did three pounds of bananas cost at the A&P store, according to a 1922 advertisement in *The Palm Beach Evening Times*?
    **A:** A quarter.

51. **Q:** On May 15, 1922, *The Tampa Times* got Florida's first license to do what?
    **A:** Operate a radio station. WDAE-AM took to the air the same day.

52. **Q:** What unusual garb was employed when three members of the Ashley gang robbed a bank in Stuart in May 1922?
    **A:** Their leader was dressed like a woman.

53. **Q:** What happened to the Ashley gang on a lonely bridge near Sebastian one night in 1924?
    **A:** The gang, which brought terror to South Florida for 14 years, was ambushed, captured, and killed by lawmen, who later said they tried to escape.

54. **Q:** What did Palm Beach County sheriff R.C. Baker declare he had destroyed 46 of in a report to federal officials on September 17, 1922?

**A:** Stills. His report on Prohibition enforcement also said he seized 95 gallons of moonshine, 232 barrels of mash and 232 gallons of other liquor; 41 people were arrested and 22 of them convicted, the report said.

55. **Q:** What pilot who later achieved fame in World War II flew from Pablo Beach— now Jacksonville Beach—to San Diego in less than 24 hours in September 1922?
    **A:** Jimmy

Jimmy Doolittle flew nonstop from Florida to California. (Acme Photo)

Doolittle's 22 1/2 hour flight, stopping only for fuel in San Antonio, Texas, established a speed record that was a far cry from the 1912 flight, which took 115 days to get to Pasadena. Jets can now make the trip in about six hours. Doolittle later led the dramatic raid on Tokyo, for which his team trained at the Panhandle's Eglin Air Force Base. He died in September 1993.

56. **Q:** What name did an Indiana-born entrepreneur give a small North Florida town that refers to people from his part of the country?
    **A:** Yankeetown, founded in 1923 by A.F. Knots, who had also founded Gary, Ind.

57. **Q:** What school of thought was barred from Florida schools by the state legislature on May 14, 1923?
    **A:** Darwin's theories of evolution.

## FLORIDA'S CHAIR OF DEATH

Florida's electric chair.
(*Miami News*)

**58. Q:** On October 7, 1924, Frank Johnson became the first person in Florida to die in what way?
**A:** In Florida's electric chair.

**59. Q:** What's the most number of people killed in Florida's electric chair in a 24-hour period?
**A:** Four. It happened three times on October 19, 1936, October 6, 1941, and March 23, 1942.

**60. Q:** How much does the state pay the person who throws the switch on Florida's electric chair?
**A:** The anonymous executioner gets $150.

**61. Q:** What happened for the first time in the South Florida city of Hialeah on January 15, 1925?
**A:** It was the first horse race at the world-famous Hialeah track.

**62. Q:** What sporting hobby did the Florida House of Representatives outlaw on May 7, 1925?
**A:** Gambling. The law declared the act a felony and called for a 5-year prison term and a $5,000 fine.

**63. Q:** In 1926, how did Hialeah Race Track get around a state ban on wagering?
**A:** It sold postcards of horses. If your horse won, the track bought the card back at a premium price that just happened to match the winning odds.

**64. Q:** What was unusual about Conner's Highway, built in 1924-1925 from the Palm Beach County coast to the Everglades farming areas?
**A:** New York businessman and South Florida winter visitor W.J. Conner built the road—now State Road 80—with his own money and charged tolls. He had bought 4,000 acres of muck land, accessible only by boat, and because development required that the property be accessible by land, he built his own road. He pushed a bill through the state legislature in two hours and 20 minutes and used dredges to build the 52-mile road in eight months for $1,800. At three cents per mile per vehicle, he collected $2,000 a year; after he died in 1929, the road was sold to the state for $660.

**65. Q:** What happened to Palm Beach's glamorous Breakers hotel on March 18, 1925?
**A:** It burned. Officials placed

losses at $7 million. Of 450 guests and 500 workers, one person died. A 610-pound man had to be lowered from his room in a large bucket. The fire was later traced to a curling iron. The hotel had also burned in 1903 and been rebuilt.

66. **Q:** What did a law passed by the Florida House of Representatives on May 13, 1925, require every day in public schools?
**A:** Bible readings.

67. **Q:** What three-time presidential candidate and key player in the 1925 "Monkey Trial" lived in Miami and was hired to pitch real estate in Coral Gables?
**A:** William Jennings Bryan, prosecutor in the infamous trial, in which a Tennessee court convicted a man of teaching evolution.

68. **Q:** In 1925, a group of bankers was invited to hold its convention in St. Petersburg. The idea was to have them enjoy fun in the sun, then go back north and rave about Florida, thus encouraging investment. What happened all week during their visit?
**A:** It was rainy and cold, and the bankers returned north and bad-mouthed Florida. It was one more nail in the coffin that was the real estate crash.

69. **Q:** What weighed 7 1/2 pounds and could be bought on a Miami street corner on July 26, 1925?
**A:** To commemorate its new building and the city's 29th anniversary, *The Miami News* published a commemorative 22-section, 504-page edition; at the time it was the fattest newspaper in world history.

Palm Beach's Breakers Hotel burns in March 1925. (*Palm Beach Post*)

70. **Q:** Why was a tree in the small southwest Florida town of LaBelle painted black in the 1920s?
**A:** A black man accused of rape was shot, then lynched at the tree in June 1926.

71. **Q:** For what purpose did the U.S. government use what is now the yacht basin at Bahia Mar in Fort Lauderdale?
**A:** It was a U.S. Coast Guard base, specializing in chasing rum runners. The city bought it in 1947.

72. **Q:** What did the U.S. Coast Guard do to Horace Alderman that has never happened since in South Florida?
**A:** The Prohibition-era rum runner was executed for killing a Coast Guard skipper, a Secret Service agent, and a machinist and wounding another man on August 7, 1927. A cutter based at the Coast Guard facility in Fort Lauderdale had intercepted him between the Florida coast and Bimini. Survivors nabbed him, and he was convicted in Miami federal court

and sentenced to be hanged, but Broward County balked. Under an obscure maritime law that called for hanging pirates at the first port reached after arrest, the Coast Guard hanged Alderman at its hangar at 6 a.m. on August 17, only 10 days after his bloody day at sea.

73. **Q:** A flight from Key West to Havana on October 28, 1927, had what historic significance?
**A:** It was the first regularly scheduled international commercial flight by an American airline. The wooden-winged 10-seater carried a crew of two and a few bags of mail over the 90-mile route in 70 minutes, averaging 85 m.p.h. The first commercial passengers flew on January 16, 1928.

74. **Q:** About 5,000 of these could be found scattered across St. Petersburg in the early part of this century. What are they?
**A:** Green benches came to symbolize the city's role as a mecca for the old. To spruce up its image, the city later phased them out. In 1987, about 100 were discovered as cheap seats at a nearby greyhound track.

75. **Q:** A St. Petersburg man said he'd uncovered an ancient Indian settlement on the Pinellas peninsula. Scientists quickly saw it was a hoax. What happened next?
**Q:** As long as they were there, they decided, they may as well dig. They then found a major archaeological site under the bones scattered by the huckster.

76. **Q:** What highway linking Florida's coasts opened April 25, 1928?

**A:** The Tamiami Trail.

77. **Q:** What did State Rep. R.E. Oliver of West Palm Beach propose in July 1928 to do to Florida?
**A:** He announced plans to introduce a bill that would split the state in half. Everything south of a line from Daytona Beach to Yankeetown would be called "South Florida," and the rest of the state would retain the "Florida" name. Oliver complained that representatives from North Florida and the Panhandle controlled the state's politics, to the detriment of the southern area.

78. **Q:** When southwest Florida developer Barron Collier grew impatient at delays in the building of the Tamiami Trail, what did he do?
**A:** He got the state legislature to carve Collier County from Lee County, and, since he owned 90 percent of the new county, arranged for its commissioners to approve $350,000 in bonds to build the road from Naples to the Dade County line.

79. **Q:** What was the nickname for opportunistic salesmen who bought land escalating in value daily during the real estate boom for a down-payment of 10 percent or less, then resold it before the original deal could be consummated and the first mortgage payment made?
**A:** Because they never spent more than the "binder" fee, they were called "binder boys." They were run out when the government started charging taxes on property's total value, not just that of the "binder."

80. **Q:** What did Fort Lauderdale pioneer Frank Stranahan do at the

New River on May 22, 1929?
**A:** He jumped. The man credited with being the city's first permanent white settler when he arrived in January 1893 was devastated by South Florida's real estate crash. He tied tiles around his waist and drowned himself. He was 65.

81. **Q:** In 1929, in Miami, Pan American Airlines began the first regularly-scheduled service between North America and what continent?
**A:** South America. The first mail flights began in 1925 and passenger flights in 1929.

82. **Q:** The giant globe that stood for years at Miami's City Hall dated to its original incarnation as what kind of facility?
**A:** It was a terminal for Pan American Airlines' seaplanes. When it opened in 1934, it was the largest seaplane base and terminal in the world. The globe was later moved to the nearby Museum of Science.

83. **Q:** What institution of higher learning was Florida's first when it opened in Palm Beach County in 1933?
**A:** Palm Beach Junior College was the state's first public junior college. It was established by the county school board to provide education for Depression-era high school graduates who could not afford to leave home for college. The school changed its named to Palm Beach Community College in 1988.

84. **Q:** What New Deal program employed 49,014 people between 1933 and 1942?
**A:** The Civilian Conservation

Corps, set up by the New Deal to supply work and hope. They planted forests, built bridges, fought fires, and helped build 12 state parks.

85. **Q:** How much did an ice cream soda with two big scoops cost at the Red Cross Drug Store in downtown Miami in May 1934?
**A:** A dime—but only on Friday and Saturday. The store later evolved into the Byrons department store.

86. **Q:** On February 15, 1933, Guiseppe Zangara's errant shot fatally injured Chicago mayor Anton Cermak at downtown Miami's bandshell. Who was Zangara's intended target?
**A:** President-elect Franklin D. Roosevelt. A woman diverted the pistol with her handbag, but five bystanders were struck by gunfire, as was Cermak. He died three weeks later. A local radio announcer thought the shots were firecrackers, signed off his broadcast and missed delivering a play-by-play on an assassination. Zangara pleaded guilty and died five weeks later, March 21, 1933, in Florida's electric chair.

87. **Q:** What happened to gangster "Ma" Barker and her son Fred at a Central Florida lakefront vacation cabin on January 16, 1935?
**A:** Led to the site by a penciled circle on a map found at a previous hideout, 15 FBI agents killed them in a 5-1/2-hour gun battle in the small town of Ocklawaha, near Ocala. Authorities later said the house had 1,500 bullet holes in it. The town's current police chief, who interviewed some of the agents, now believes the Barkers

were killed in the first 45 minutes
and jumpy feds continued to shoot
sporadically for hours at anything
that moved.

88. **Q:** In 1936, Seminole Indians,
reeling with the rest of the country
under the Depression,
had a historic meeting in
the Everglades with Gov.
David Sholtz. To his
offers of help they
replied, *"pohoan
checkish."* What did
that mean?
**A:** "Leave us alone."

Depression-era
Governor David
Sholtz.

# 16
## History:
## Modern Florida
### (Since 1941)

1. **Q:** What was Florida's population rank at the beginning of World War II?
   **A:** It was 27th. By 1950 it was 20th. By 1960 it was 10th.

The bustling Florida East Coast railway station in Miami, 1940. (Historical Museum of Southern Florida)

2. **Q:** What did future president George Bush do at Lake Okeechobee in the 1940s?
   **A:** He flew training missions over it as a Navy pilot.

3. **Q:** What kind of enemy vessel, captured off Pearl Harbor in 1941, is now in a Key West museum?

**A:** A two-man Japanese submarine. It is now in the museum at the old Key West lighthouse.

4. **Q:** What did the U.S. military do to Frostproof at least twice during World War II?
   **A:** They bombed it. The town is near Avon Park Bombing Range, and at night, training pilots sometimes mistook its lit intersection as a target marker.

5. **Q:** Twenty-three citizens of what country are buried at the city cemetery in Arcadia?
   **A:** The graves hold British pilots killed while training in Florida during World War II. Each Memorial Day, hundreds of Americans, British, Canadians, and others assemble to honor them.

6. **Q:** What key American military mission during World War II was trained for at Eglin Air Force base in the Panhandle?
   **A:** Gen. Jimmy Doolittle's raid on Tokyo.

## THE WAR OFF OUR SHORE

7. **Q:** In June 1942, a group came ashore at Ponte Vedra Beach, near Jacksonville, on an evil mission. Who were they?
   **A:** Nazi saboteurs. Their plan was to blow up defense plants and destroy important highways. They were betrayed by members of a second deployment at Long Island and eventually captured. Six were executed; the other two, who had cooperated with authorities, went to prison and were deported back to Germany after the war.

8. **Q:** During World War II, groups of citizens sprang up to man viewing stations and scan the waters off Florida's coasts with binoculars. What were they watching for?
   **A:** German submarines.

9. **Q:** Why were South Florida oceanfront hotels asked to dim lights during World War II?
   **A:** Their lights silhouetted merchant ships and made them sitting ducks for the German submarines that sank many of them. The hotels complained the ban on lights would hurt the tourist business.

10. **Q:** During World War II, what kind of facility in Central Florida was one of 151 in the country to provide alternative service for conscientious objectors?
    **A:** A privy factory.

11. **Q:** On a small Pacific island during World War II, Ernest Ivy "Boots" Thomas of Monticello took part in an act that became a symbol of the American fighting spirit. What did he do?
    **A:** He helped raise the American flag at Iwo Jima on February 23, 1945. Five days later Thomas, a week shy of 21, died in battle.

12. **Q:** A base for what kind of air vehicle was destroyed by fire during a hurricane on September 15, 1945?

**A:** Blimps. The base, built in 1942, featured three wooden hangars 16-1/2 stories high and more than 1,000 feet long. Lost in the fire and 170-m.p.h. winds were 368 military and civilian aircraft and 28 blimps. The site now hosts Miami's Metrozoo.

13. **Q:** What actor judged a University of Florida beauty contest at the request of 1947 yearbook editor Patrick O'Neal, who himself later became an actor?
    **A:** Ronald Reagan.

14. **Q:** What kind of person enrolled at the University of Florida for the first time in 1947?
    **A:** Women. About 600 enrolled that year.

15. **Q:** What was Florida State University called until 1947?
    **A:** Florida State College for Women.

**16. Q:** The Long Range Proving Ground, created by President Truman on May 11, 1949, was predecessor to what?
**A:** The Kennedy Space Center. The proving ground later became nearby Patrick Air Force Base.

**17. Q:** What left Cape Canaveral for the first time ever on July 24, 1950?
**A:** A German V-2 became the first rocket ever launched by the United States.

**18. Q:** What happened to civil rights leader Harry Moore and his wife on Christmas Day, 1951, at their home in Mims, near Melbourne?
**A:** The two were fatally injured when a bomb exploded under their bed. It was their 25th wedding anniversary. Moore had founded the northern Brevard County chapter of the National Association for the Advancement of Colored People (NAACP) in 1934. He later started other chapters around the state and became state president in 1941. In 1979, a former Marine claimed he had made the bomb at the request of Central Florida Ku Klux Klan members and former Lake County sheriff Willis McCall.

**19. Q:** What future revolutionary leader appealed for money at the Flagler Theater in downtown Miami in 1953?
**A:** Fidel Castro. Six years later, in the early morning hours of January 1, 1959, he seized Cuba from Fulgencio Batista.

Cuban leader Fidel Castro. (CNN)

**20. Q:** What happened to Palm Beach County Circuit Judge C.E. Chillingworth and his wife on June 15, 1955?
**A:** They were murdered. Two men later confessed to taking them out to sea and dumping them overboard on behalf of Municipal Judge Joseph A. Peel, allegedly because Chillingworth was cracking down on Peel's gambling connections.

**21. Q:** What ill-fated military operation organized in Miami was launched April 17, 1961?
**A:** The Bay of Pigs invasion of Cuba. Designed to overthrow premier Fidel Castro, it ended in disaster. Nearly 1,300 members of Brigade 2506 went ashore; 114 were killed and the remainder imprisoned after promised U.S. air cover never came.

**22. Q:** What did Alan B. Shepard, Jr. do on May 5, 1961, in Florida that no American had ever done before?
**A:** Leaving from Cape Canaveral, he was the first American in space.

Alan Shepard, the first American in space. (NASA)

**23. Q:** What remnant of the early 20th century was mothballed in the North Florida town of Perry on August 31, 1961?
**A:** The town's telephone system became the last in Florida to abandon cranks for dials.

24. **Q:** Why were U.S. battle jets secretly sent to Key West on October 6, 1962?
    **A:** Squadrons of the U.S. Navy's fastest jet fighters were assigned to Boca Chica Naval Air Station as the Cuban missile crisis escalated.

25. **Q:** What was the name Cape Canaveral changed to on November 28, 1963?
    **A:** Cape Kennedy. It reverted to its original name in 1973 and the space facility on it was named Kennedy Space Center.

26. **Q:** What happened to civil rights leader Dr. Martin Luther King, Jr., on June 11, 1964, in St. Augustine?
    **A:** He was arrested for refusing to leave the steps of a motel restaurant. King had come to the historic city to spearhead a program of protests and marches to press for desegregation.

27. **Q:** What did the federal government try to build from Palatka to the Gulf of Mexico in the 1960s?
    **A:** The Cross-Florida Barge Canal. It was killed by environmentalists in the 1970s. Efforts to turn the dry beds into park land got underway in the early 1990s.

The Cross-Florida Barge Canal, 1966.

28. **Q:** What happened on January 27, 1967—19 years and one day earlier—less than a mile from where *Challenger* exploded in 1986?
    **A:** Three astronauts died when fire swept an Apollo spaceship on a launch pad.

29. **Q:** What happened at Cape Canaveral on July 16, 1969?
    **A:** Apollo 11 lifted off on its way to man's first landing on the moon.

Apollo 11 leaves Florida for a rendezvous with the moon, July 16, 1969. (NASA)

30. **Q:** Why didn't unlucky Apollo 13, which left from Florida's Cape Kennedy on April 11, 1970, fulfill its mission?
    **A:** Man's third attempt to land on the moon was aborted in open space when an oxygen tank exploded. The three-man crew crawled into the now-unnecessary lunar landing module and rode the crippled craft home.

**31.  Q:** Who placed a historical marker honoring slain Vietnam soldier Leon Hunt in Fort Lauderdale's Holiday Park?
**A:** His parents.

**32.  Q:** What did Cuba's Fidel Castro end on April 6, 1973?
**A:** The Freedom Flights to Miami, which had brought 261,000 people to freedom since 1965.

**33.  Q:** What happened to two girls at Florida State University's Chi Omega sorority house on January 7, 1978?
**A:** The two were murdered. Ted Bundy was later accused of the crime and several murders across the country. He was convicted in the Florida State murders and was sentenced to death on September 30, 1979. After an 11-year stretch of delays and appeals that came to symbolize the lengthy death penalty process, Bundy died in Florida's electric chair on January 24, 1989.

**34.  Q:** What modern new state building was dedicated March 31, 1978?
**A:** The 22-story new capitol building.

In the years following the revolution, Cubans fled to Florida by air or by sea (September 1966 photo). (U.S. Coast Guard)

**35.  Q:** When Florida's new capitol building was opened in 1978, what was done with the old building?
**A:** The 1845 capitol was restored to its 1902 appearance and has been turned into a state historic museum.

**36.  Q:** What religious ceremony was celebrated in 1978 in Miami's Orange Bowl?
**A:** A bar mitzvah reception. A 64-piece marching band, waiters dressed as referees, and waitresses dressed as cheerleaders all led local Rabbi Irving Lehrman to remark that the event was more "bar" than "mitzvah."

**37.  Q:** To dramatize an ambitious cleanup of industrial Jacksonville's air and water, what brave act did Mayor Hans Tanzler perform in 1978?

The new Capitol building, dedicated in March 1978, hosts the inauguration of Gov. Bob Graham in January 1979.

**A:** He took a dip in the St. Johns River, which in the past had been so filthy that most swimmers would not have gone near it.

38. **Q:** Where did Nicaraguan leader Anastasio Somoza go when he fled his homeland and the Sandinistas on July 17, 1979?
    **A:** Miami.

Nicaraguan president Anastasio Somoza fled to exile in Florida in 1979.

39. **Q:** What happened to the South Florida community of Andytown on November 1, 1979?
    **A:** The tiny settlement—nothing more than a restaurant bar and gas station at U.S. 27 and Alligator Alley— closed down. Founded by a Greek immigrant in 1947, the town never had more than 11 residents. It was bought out by the state for an Interstate 75 interchange. Andytown's Greek-American owners threw a bash and vowed to return.

40. **Q:** What happened to the U.S. Coast Guard cutter *Blackthorn* on January 28, 1980?
    **A:** The ship struck the freighter *Capricorn* and sank in Tampa Bay, killing 23 crewmen.

41. **Q:** What failed 1980 rescue mission in the Middle East is memorialized at Hurlburt Field in the Panhandle?
    **A:** The April 1980 attempt to rescue American hostages from Iran. Five of the eight soldiers killed and many of the injured were from Hurlburt.

42. **Q:** What event began in the Cuban port town of Mariel in April 1980?
    **A:** The exodus of about 120,000 Cubans to South Florida, known as the Mariel boatlift.

43. **Q:** What did a freighter strike in Tampa Bay in a blinding rainstorm on May 9, 1980, leading to 35 deaths?
    **A:** The Sunshine Skyway bridge. A quarter-mile piece of the bridge, which connects the Pinellas peninsula with the mainland to the south, fell into the bay, taking three cars with it. Within minutes four more vehicles and a Greyhound bus with 26 passengers drove off the span.

44. **Q:** What court action on May 18, 1980, sparked three days of deadly riots in Miami's Liberty City?
    **A:** The acquittal of five Dade County policemen in the beating death of a black man. The violence left 18 dead and $100 million in property damage.

45. **Q:** When the Sunshine Skyway bridge over Tampa Bay collapsed in 1980, most Miami-area media were able to cover it because they were already in Tampa covering what?
    **A:** The trial of Dade County policemen in the death of a black man. The trial had been moved because of pre-trial publicity. The officers' acquittal led to Miami's 1980 riots.

46. **Q:** What left Cape Canaveral on April 12, 1981?
    **A:** *Columbia*, the first space shuttle. It would fly 28 missions in 22 years before it came apart on reentry on February 1, 2003, killing the seven astronauts aboard.

47. **Q:** What 6-year-old Hollywood boy's gruesome murder in 1981

sparked a national movement to protect children?

**A:** Adam Walsh. The boy disappeared from a department store in July 1981; 16 days later his remains were found in a canal along Florida's Turnpike near Vero Beach. To date, the murder has not been solved. Walsh's parents later founded the Adam Walsh Foundation for Missing and Exploited Children.

48. **Q:** On October 26, 1981, 33 of 67 boat people desperately seeking new lives drowned when their boat broke up less than a mile off Hillsboro Beach, north of Fort Lauderdale. From what impoverished country had they come?
**A:** Haiti.

49. **Q:** What happened to Arcadia native Gen. James Dozier on December 17, 1981?
**A:** The U.S. general was kidnapped in Italy by the Red Brigade. He was freed in a commando raid on January 28, 1982.

50. **Q:** On October 18, 1982, at Orlando International Airport, two of what unique airplane landed simultaneously?
**A:** Two Concordes, one from British Airways and one from Air France, landed side by side. The publicity stunt took place at the Orlando airport because the former military air base had extremely long runways.

51. **Q:** The June 1983 mission of the space shuttle *Challenger* was a first for what American astronaut?
**A:** It carried Sally Ride, the first American woman in space.

52. **Q:** In July 1985, salvager Mel Fisher, diving on the ocean bottom near Key West, located what may

The last crew of the space shuttle *Challenger*. (NASA)

be the richest of what kind of find?
**A:** He found probably the world's largest sunken treasure: the main cargo of the Spanish ship *Nuestra Señora de Atocha*, which sank on September 6, 1622. Its value is estimated at nearly $400 million, mainly in silver bars.

53. **Q:** What happened at the Kennedy Space Center on January 28, 1986?
**A:** The space shuttle *Challenger* exploded 74 seconds after takeoff, killing seven astronauts.

54. **Q:** How much money did the license plate commemorating the fatal 1986 explosion of the space shuttle *Challenger* make in its first three months of issue?
**A:** $1 million. The proceeds go to an astronauts' memorial at Kennedy Space Center.

55. **Q:** For more than 75 years, what would *The St. Petersburg Evening Independent* do any day the sun never shined?
**A:** The newspaper was given away free. The practice began on September 20, 1910, and ended when the newspaper published its last edition on November 7, 1986.

56. **Q:** At what majestic historic mansion near downtown Miami did

Miami's Vizcaya hosted President Reagan and Pope John Paul II in 1987. (Vizcaya)

President Ronald Reagan and Pope John Paul II meet on September 10, 1987, during the pope's visit to South Florida?
**A:** At Vizcaya, the stunning 34-room mansion built by 1,000 workers from 1914 to 1916 for James Deering, of the International Harvester farm machine empire. *Vizcaya* is a Basque word meaning "elevated place." The house is now a museum.

57.  **Q:** What vice did the state of Florida start practicing itself in January 1988?
     **A:** Gambling. The state lottery started with scratch-off instant-win cards and moved a few months later to a statewide drawing.

58.  **Q:** In 1988, the lighthouse at Egmont Key, south of St. Petersburg in Tampa Bay, ceased being the only lighthouse in Florida with what?
     **A:** People. It was the last of the state's 23 lighthouses to automate.

59.  **Q:** What headline appeared on the front page of *The Miami News* on December 31, 1988?
     **A:** ``Farewell, Miami.'' After 92

years, South Florida's oldest newspaper—founded on May 15, 1896—was hampered by declining readership and financial losses. It printed its last edition on New Year's Eve, 1988.

60.  **Q:** How did Florida rank among the fastest-growing states in the 1980s?
     **A:** It was the fourth fastest growing state, with a 32.8 percent change between 1980 and 1990. Tops were Nevada (50), Alaska (36.9), and Arizona (34.8). From 1990 to 2000 census, it was seventh, behind several western states and Georgia.

61.  **Q:** How many Floridians were over the age of 65 in the year 2000?
     **A:** According to the U.S. census of 2000, 17.6 percent. The percentage of persons under the age of five years was 5.9. The total number of people claiming residence in 2000 was 15,982,378. And for 2003 it was up to 17,019,068.

62.  **Q:** What is Florida's current population rank?
     **A:** It's fourth, behind New York, California, and Texas. It is projected to pass New York into third place by 2015.

63.  **Q:** When Panamanian strongman Manuel Noriega surrendered in January 1990, to what American installation was he flown?
     **A:** Homestead Air Force Base.

Former Panamani
strong man Manu
Noriega in custod

**64. Q:** According to the 2000 census, what fraction of Floridians were natives?
**A:** Less than a third: 32.7 percent. It was 35 percent in the 1990 census.

## HURRICANES

**66. Q:** Why was August 24, 1992, a black day for most South Floridians?
**A:** It's the day Hurricane Andrew struck, killing 26, leaving thousands homeless and causing billions of dollars' worth of damage. For the storm's 10th anniversary, in 2002, the National Hurricane Center officially changed its category from 4 to 5 on the Saffir-Simpson scale of hurricane strength. The center said new research indicated top sustained winds were not 140 to 150 mph, but rather 165 mph.

**67. Q:** What was unusual about the 2004 hurricane season?
**A:** Florida was hit by a remarkable four hurricanes in the same year—not just that, but all in six weeks' time. Only once before had four hurricanes struck a state the same year: Texas in 1886. Charley struck Punta Gorda on Aug. 13. Frances struck near Stuart on Sept. 5. Ivan struck on the Florida-Alabama line, west of Pensacola, on Sept. 16. And Jeanne struck near Stuart on Sept. 25.

**68. Q:** What was special about the landfalls of Hurricanes Frances and Jeanne in 2004?
**A:** They struck virtually the same spot, and at almost the same hour and day of the week, within three weeks of each

**65. Q:** How many times over did Florida's population increase between the beginning of World War II and 2003?
**A:** It increased more than 11-fold, from 1.9 million in 1940 to an estimated 17 million in 2003.

other. Frances struck Sewall's Point, south of Stuart, at about 1 A.M. on Sunday, Sept. 5. Jeanne struck about two miles east of that, at the south end of Hutchinson Island, at about 11:50 P.M. on Saturday, Sept. 25.

**69. Q:** What was the total insured damage from the four hurricanes that struck in 2004?
**A:** Anywhere from $26 billion to $30 billion: Charley, $6.8 billion; Frances, $4 billion to $8 billion; Ivan, up to $10 billion; and Jeanne, about $6 billion. Andrew did $16 billion damage in 1992, but researchers said in 2004 that, when taking into account inflation and growth along the coast, they believe a hurricane like Andrew would do as much as $45 billion in damage now.

**70. Q:** How much of Florida got at least one of the four hurricanes in 2004?
**A:** Every county in Florida received at least tropical storm–strength winds. Thirty-seven of the state's 67 counties got hurricane-force winds at least once. Several counties were hit three times—by Charley, from the south or west, and then by Frances or Jeanne, from the east.

# 17

## Florida Stew

1. **Q:** What's the origin of the term "Florida Cracker"?
   **A:** The term, usually referring to a rural old-timer and often offensive, stems from Florida's old Wild West days, when the state's cowboys drove the herds to market, cracking their 18-foot whips at the dogies to move them along. It has also been attributed to dried food poor people brought with them when they traveled to Florida.

2. **Q:** What nickname is given to residents of Key West?
   **A:** "Conchs" (pronounced KONKS), for the giant shellfish that is a local delicacy.

3. **Q:** What shows a sunrise/sunset, a sabal palm, a steamboat, and an Indian woman scattering flowers?
   **A:** Florida's official state seal.

4. **Q:** What geographic error did the first state seal display?
   **A:** It showed a mountainous background, far from appropriate for flat Florida.

5. **Q:** What was wrong with the Indian headdress on the first official state seal?

**A:** A woman was wearing it. Only Indian males wore headdresses.

Florida's politically-corrected state seal. (Florida Secretary of State)

6. **Q:** What's unusual about the designation of the moonstone as Florida's official state gem?
   **A:** It is not naturally found in Florida—nor was it found on the moon. The designation honors America's moon missions, which left from Florida's Kennedy Space Center.

7. **Q:** What's Florida's official state tree?
   **A:** The sabal palm.

8. **Q:** What's the official state flower?

A: The orange blossom.

9. Q: What's the official state beverage?
A: Orange juice, of course.

10. Q: What's the official state song?
A: Stephen F. Foster's "Old Folks at Home," best known for its opening line: "Way down upon the Swanee river . . ."

11. Q: What was unusual about Stephen F. Foster's selection for his song "Old Folks at Home"?
A: He never saw North Florida's Suwannee river. His brother picked it from an atlas for its melodic name, which Stephen Foster shortened for the song. He rejected their first choices, South Carolina's Pee Dee and Mississippi's Yazoo.

12. Q: Florida's official state bird holds the same honor in four other states. What is it?
A: The mockingbird, state bird in Florida, Texas, Arkansas, Mississippi, and Tennessee.

13. Q: What's the official state animal?
A: The endangered Florida panther.

14. Q: What's the official state salt-water mammal?
A: The dolphin, perhaps as much a symbol of Florida as the flamingo. Sailors considered the presence of dolphins near their boats a sign of good luck.

15. Q: What's the official state fresh-water mammal?

A: The endangered manatee, or sea cow.

16. Q: What's the official state salt-water fish?
A: The sailfish.

17. Q: What's the official state fresh-water fish?
A: The largemouth bass.

18. Q: How many ships have carried the official name *Florida*?
A: Ten, ranging from a wind-powered 1820s sloop to a Trident-class nuclear submarine commissioned in 1983.

19. Q: What was ironic about the side-wheel steamer *U.S.S. Florida*, which served from 1862 to 1864?
A: The federal ship was used by the Union to help blockade the Confederacy's coasts, including that of the state for which it was named.

20. Q: What is the official state play?
A: *The Cross and the Sword*, a story of the exploration and initial settlement of Florida. It is performed nightly in the summertime in St. Augustine.

21. Q: What are the state's three biggest public colleges and their locations?
A: As of 2000, they were: University of Florida, Gainesville (50,041); University of South Florida, Tampa (35,473); Florida State University, Tallahassee (33,587).

22. Q: Where's Florida Atlantic University?
A: Boca Raton.

23. Q: What city hosts two major state universities?

Florida A&M's famous marching band. *(Miami News)*

A: Tallahassee: Florida State and Florida A&M.

24. Q: Florida International University in Miami is the home of a center for the study of exiles from what country?
A: Cuba.

25. Q: What did Fort Lauderdale city fathers leave untouched for six unbroken miles?
A: The beach. In a move rare for Florida, the city banned buildings on the east side of State Road A1A, leaving a 6-mile stretch of open beach.

26. Q: Who owns the beach?
A: From the "mean high tide line" to the water, every inch of beach is owned by the state of Florida. The line is an imaginary border determined after a 19-year study by the state Department of Natural Resources, and is often impossible to determine without a survey.

27. Q: How does the Everglades rank in size among national parks?
A: With 1.4 million acres, or 2,187 square miles, it's bigger than Delaware. It's third among national parks in the lower 48 states, behind only Yellowstone, with 9,250 square miles—nearly the size of Virginia—and Death Valley with 5,219 square miles. Six parks in Alaska are bigger.

28. Q: Florida has two national parks. One is Everglades. What's the other?
A: Biscayne National Park, established in 1968, covers more than 283 square miles, encompassing 44 islands and a large chunk of southern Biscayne Bay. More than 90 percent is underwater. The park's entrance is near Homestead.

29. Q: What fraction of the cocaine entering the U.S. is believed to pass through Florida?
A: The figure has dropped from 70 percent in the mid-1990s to only about 30 percent; much of the traffic has shifted to the southwestern United States.

30. Q: What do state prisoners at Union Correctional Institute in North Florida make about 25,000

of every day?
A: License plates. Each prisoner earns 55 cents to $1.10 per hour making the plates.

31. Q: Before county names were placed on Florida license plates, how were they identified by county?
A: Each county was assigned a number, which was the first one or two digits on the license. For example, Dade was 1, Broward 10, and Palm Beach, 6.

32. In which decade, since the census began in 1840, did Florida's population undergo the most dramatic increase?
A: Between 1950 and 1960, the state's population increased a staggering 78.7 percent.

33. Q: As of Veterans Day 1993, only 5,636 veterans of what conflict were still alive in Florida?
A: They were the only World War I veterans left in Florida, and among only 30,000 to 38,000 nationwide, to note the 75th anniversary of the end of The Great War on November 11, 1918. The average age in 1993 was 97. By 2002, fewer than 200 veterans of the war remained nationwide. Officials did not have an estimate for Florida.

34. Q: Where's America's largest Jewish population group outside New York City?
A: Southeast Florida. As of 1992, 515,000 of the nation's six million Jews were estimated to live in Dade, Broward, and Palm Beach counties.

35. Q: Who is the unlikely owner of the 300,000-acre Deseret ranch in Central Florida?

A: The Church of Jesus Christ of Latter-Day Saints—the Mormons.

36. Q: As of March 2003, what Florida cities had daily newspapers with Sunday circulation above 200,000?
A: Seven. In order: St. Petersburg *(Times)*, Miami *(Herald)*, Orlando *(Sentinel)*, Fort Lauderdale *(South Florida Sun-Sentinel)*, Tampa *(Tribune)*, West Palm Beach *(Palm Beach Post)*, and Jacksonville *(Florida Times-Union)*.

37. Q: What supermarket tabloid wss published for decades in Lantana, near West Palm Beach?
A: The *National Enquirer*. It moved from New York in 1971 and left Lantana for nearby Boca Raton in 2000. A year later, an anthrax attack killed one worker and the contaminated building was shut down.

38. Q: How many nuclear power plant complexes are in Florida?
A: Three: Turkey Point (two plants), south of Miami; St. Lucie (two plants), south of Fort Pierce; and Crystal River, north of Tampa.

39. Q: What kind of show do the Pensacola-based Blue Angels perform?
A: They fly jet planes. The U.S. Navy's jet plane demonstration squadron is based at the U.S.

The U.S. Navy's Blue Angels jet squadron. (U.S. Navy)

Naval Air Station in Pensacola.

40. **Q:** What kind of facility was built at the U.S. Coast Guard station on Peanut Island, just off Palm Beach, for then-president and part-time Palm Beach resident John F. Kennedy?
**A:** A fallout shelter. The underground facility, to be used in case of a nuclear attack, was built during the Cuban missile crisis.

41. **Q:** What's the name for the 1930s tropical pastel architectural style so prevalent in one section of Miami Beach that the area has been named a national historic site?
**A:** Art Deco. The 800 buildings in lower Miami Beach represent the largest concentration of art deco architecture in the world. The style is depicted by sleek building designs, light colors, neon, and flamingos.

42. **Q:** What's the name for the railed system that moves people around downtown Miami?
**A:** The Metromover.

43. **Q:** What's the name of South Florida's railed rapid transit system?
**A:** Metrorail.

44. **Q:** What specialty found in South Florida Cuban restaurants is a combination of saffron, rice, shrimp, and chicken?
**A:** Paella.

45. **Q:** What would a fancy restaurant call swamp cabbage, the delicacy for which the southwest Florida town of LaBelle holds a festival every year?
**A:** Heart of palm. It's the heart of a palm tree.

46. **Q:** Where is the largest tropical botanical garden in the continental United States?
**A:** It's the 83-acre Fairchild Tropical Gardens in Coral Gables. The garden was devastated by Hurricane Andrew, which destroyed more than 2,000 trees. It is slowly recovering.

47. **Q:** What unusual camp will you find in Titusville?
**A:** A space camp. The camp, which opened in 1988 with a first-summer group of 2,700, is one of only two in the country. The Florida camp closed in the fall of 2002. The other is at the Marshall Space Center in Huntsville, Ala.

48. **Q:** Why was April 11, 1986, the bloodiest day in FBI history?
**A:** Two agents were killed and five others hurt in a quiet suburban Miami neighborhood in a shootout with two men suspected in at least six robberies. The suspects were also killed in the 10-minute gun battle.

49. **Q:** In 1976, Melbourne-area school-children raised money to buy an uncracked, life-sized replica of what item from American history?
**A:** The Liberty Bell. The model, bought from the same company that made the original bell, stands in the Liberty Bell Museum, just west of the Melbourne Auditorium.

50. **Q:** What does the Florida Highway Patrol Troop K patrol?
**A:** Florida's Turnpike.

51. **Q:** What can you not do on the side of the road on Florida's Turnpike?
**A:** Hitchhike.

52. **Q:** What's the most popular candy

sold along Florida's Turnpike?
A: Snickers.

53. Q: What did a 1979 Florida Supreme Court decision allow in state courtrooms?
A: Journalists' television and still cameras and recording devices.

54. Q: Although it is a long way from the open sea, where in Tallahassee can you find treasure from ship-wrecks?
A: The Florida Museum of History, which tells the story of Florida from the time of its earliest inhabitants to the present.

55. Q: Where's the largest air force base in what used to be called "the free world"?
A: Eglin Air Force Base, in the Panhandle. It's two-thirds the size of Rhode Island.

56. Q: What government installation covers the lower end of the Interbay Peninsula, which juts from downtown Tampa into Tampa Bay?
A: MacDill Air Force Base.

57. Q: In what Florida city was the Persian Gulf Fleet's headquarters during the Persian Gulf War?
A: Tampa.

58. Q: According to a 1989 study by the Federal Emergency Management Agency, 68 places in Florida were potential targets for what?
A: Soviet nuclear attack. Primary targets were military installations and support industries, political centers, ports, and power plants.

59. Q: How much is Florida's personal state income tax?
A: It is one of only a few states in the country without one.

60. Q: According to the old song, you would see the moon over what Florida city?
A: "Moon over Miami."

61. Q: How many Canadians visit Florida every year?
A: About 2.4 million—one in 11 Canadians.

62. Q: What does Florida's "bed tax" tax?
A: It's a special tax surcharge for people staying in hotels.

63. Q: What South Florida town's buildings were designed after Arabian fables?
A: Opa-locka, a suburb of Miami, was built in 1926 with domes, spires, and parapets to recreate the *Thousand and One Nights* tales of Arabian folklore. The main streets, laid out in the shape of a crescent moon, are named for characters in the tales.

64. Q: What new area code was established in 1988 and what area does it cover?
A: 407: Orlando.

65. Q: How many area codes does Florida have?
A: When three-digit area codes were established in 1947, Florida had one: 305. It split off 813 for the Gulf area in 1953 and 904 for North Florida in 1965. That lasted until 1988, when 407 was established from Boca Raton to Orlando. In the years that followed, those four area codes grew to 18. The culprits: FAX machines, pagers, and of course, cell phones.

66. Q: The Palace Saloon, which claims to be the oldest tavern in Florida, is in what historic seaside town?
A: Fernandina Beach.

67. **Q:** What religious center in St. Leo, north of Tampa, is the only one in Florida?
    **A:** The St. Leo Abbey, more than a century old, is Florida's only monastery. In 1988 it housed 48 monks, with former occupations that included mailman, insurance clerk, real estate agent, and country music disc jockey. In February 2004, a small group of Catholic monks said they would have the state's second monastery operating by the end of the year.

68. **Q:** What word did poet Ralph Waldo Emerson use to describe North Florida's St. Johns River?
    **A:** "Grotesque."

69. **Q:** Where was Dade County's first courthouse?
    **A:** Juno. From 1889 to 1899, the settlement was the county seat of Dade County, which then included present-day Palm Beach County. It later moved to Miami.

70. **Q:** Why won't you find the Dade County town of Islandia on a map?
    **A:** It never was. Founded in 1960 on 33 islands southeast of downtown Miami, the offshore city was to house a resort rivaling Miami Beach. Environmentalists quashed the plan and the "city" is now part of Biscayne National Park.

71. **Q:** Why can't you bicycle on Looe Key?
    **A:** The entire key is underwater. Once a 900-foot by 300-foot island, it was the refuge for the crew of the British frigate *H.M.S. Looe* when it wrecked on a nearby reef in 1744. The key eventually eroded until now only at extreme low tides do even the tops of rocks or coral heads surface. It is now a national marine sanctuary.

72. **Q:** Why are there no back yards in South Florida's Stiltsville community?
    **A:** The homes are on stilts in the middle of Biscayne Bay. The area became part of Biscayne National Park in 1980. Seven of the 14 buildings were destroyed by Hurricane Andrew in 1992. The rest were to be phased out by 1999, but in 2003, the federal government said it might keep them around for public access.

73. **Q:** Where will you be if you're at Calle Ocho?
    **A:** Spanish for "Eighth Street," it's just that—Southwest Eighth Street in Little Havana, near downtown Miami. The street has become as famous an artery for South Florida's expatriate Cuban community as Broadway is for New Yorkers or Hollywood Boulevard is for film buffs.

74. **Q:** Why do up to a million people crowd Southwest Eighth Street every year?
    **A:** For the Calle Ocho Festival, America's largest Hispanic celebration.

75. **Q:** Four different people with the same famous profession wintered at the Cocolobo Club on tiny Adams Key, now part of the Biscayne National Park near Miami. What was their occupation?
    **A:** Four presidents—Warren Harding, Herbert Hoover, Lyndon

Johnson, and Richard Nixon— vacationed at the 28-acre island.

76. **Q:** Each state is allowed to place two statues in the nation's capitol in Washington, D.C. Which Floridians are so honored?
**A:** Dr. John Gorrie of Apalachicola, whose inventions led to air conditioning, and Edmund K. Smith of Palatka, the last Confederate general to surrender in the Civil War.

77. **Q:** What fraction of Floridians lives in South Florida?
**A:** Nearly one in four—23.6 percent—live in Dade or Broward counties. Add Palm Beach County and it jumps to nearly 31 percent— almost one in three.

78. **Q:** What's the greatest cause of death in Florida?
**A:** Cardiovascular diseases killed 38.7 percent of the 167,181 people who died in Florida in 2001. Cancer was second with 23.2 percent. No other causes come close; HIV, the virus that causes AIDS, killed 0.6 percent, homicide 1 percent.

79. **Q:** What fraction of Floridians lives below the poverty level?
**A:** According to 2000 U.S. census figures, about 2 million people— 12.6 percent of Floridians—were below the threshold.

80. **Q:** What fraction of Florida's housing units is mobile homes?
**A:** While the number increased by more than 86,000 between 1990 and 2000, the percentage dropped from 12.5 percent to 11.6 percent. But Florida continues to lead the nation. Its 842,701 units made up close to 10 percent.

81. **Q:** How many counties in Florida are "dry"?
**A:** Six Florida counties forbid the sale of beverages containing more than 6.243 percent alcohol.

82. **Q:** According to tradition, what happens once you get sand in your shoes?
**A:** You are hooked on Florida. You'll be back soon. Or you may never leave.

# *Selected Bibliography*

**Q:** Want to learn more?
**A:** Here's how

Most of the following books, newspapers, or agencies were heavily used as sources in *Florida Fun Facts.* A few others are included because they will lead you into further fun-facts journeys. You may want to explore them to learn more about Florida.

## BOOKS:

American Automobile Association, *Florida Tourbook,* published annually, Heathrow, Fla., American Automobile Association

Bicentennial Commission of Florida, *The Florida Bicentennial Trail: A Heritage Revisited,* 1976, Tallahassee, State of Florida

Boone, Floyd E., *Boone's Florida Historical Markers and Sites,* 1988, Moore Haven, Rainbow Books

Burnett, Gene, *Florida's Past: People and Events that Shaped the State, Volumes 1-3,* 1986, 1988, 1991, Sarasota, Pineapple Press

Douglas, Marjory Stoneman, *The Everglades: River of Grass,* 1947, Sarasota, Pineapple Press

Federal Writers' Project, Florida: *A Guide to the Southernmost State,* 1939, New York, Oxford University Press

Florida Department of Commerce, Division of Tourism, *Florida Vacation Guide,* published annually, Tallahassee, Florida Department of Commerce

Gill, Joan E., and Beth R. Read, Editors, *Born of the Sun: The Official Florida Bicentennial Commemorative Book,*1975, Hollywood, Worth International Communications Corp

Henry, James A., Kenneth M. Portier, and Jan Coyne, *The Climate and Weather of Florida,* 1994, Sarasota, Pineapple Press

Kale, Herbert W. III, and David S. Maehr, *Florida's Birds,* 1990, Sarasota, Pineapple Press

Kennedy, Stetson, *Palmetto Country,* 1942, Tallahassee, Florida A&M University Press

Kleinberg, Howard, *Miami, The Way We Were,* 1989, Tampa, Surfside Publishing

LaFreniere, Ed and Barbara, *Complete Guide to Life in Florida,* 1995, Sarasota, Pineapple Press

Mahon, John, *History of the Second Seminole War, 1835-1842,* 1968, Gainesville, University of Florida Press

Marth, Del and Martha J., *The Florida Almanac,* published biennially since 1972, Suwannee River Press, Branford, Florida

McCarthy, Kevin M., Editor, *The Book Lover's Guide to Florida,* 1992, Sarasota, Pineaple Press

McIver, Stuart, *Dreamers, Schemers and Scalawags: The Florida Chronicles Vol. 1,* 1994, Sarasota, Pineapple Press

McIver, Stuart, *Glimpses of South Florida History,* 1988, Miami, Florida Flair Books

Morris, Allen, *The Florida Handbook*, published biennially since 1947, Tallahassee, Peninsular Publishing Company

Nelson, Gil, *The Trees of Florida*, 1994, Sarasota, Pineapple Press

O'Sullivan, Maurice, and Jack C. Lane, Editors, *The Florida Reader: Visions of Paradise from 1530 to the Present*, 1991, Sarasota, Pineapple Press

Stamm, Doug, *The Springs of Florida*, 1994, Sarasota, Pineapple Press

Tebeau, Charlton W. and Ruby Leach Carson, *Florida: From Indian Trail to Space Age*, 1965, Delray Beach, Southern Publishing

Tebeau, Charlton W., *A History of Florida*, 1971, Coral Gables, University of Miami Press

Zoretich, Frank, *Cheap Thrills Florida (The Bottom Half)*, 1994, Sarasota, Pineapple Press

## NEWSPAPERS

*The Palm Beach Post*, 2751 S. Dixie Highway, West Palm Beach 33405. Attention: News Library

*South Florida Sun-Sentinel*, 200 E. Los Olas Blvd., Fort Lauderdale 33301

*Miami Herald*, One Herald Plaza, Miami 33125

## AGENCIES

**Florida Department of Commerce**, Collins Building, Tallahassee 32399-2000 (Florida Official Transportation Map)

**Florida Department of Natural Resources,** Division of Recreation and Parks, Marjory Stoneman Douglas Building, 3900 Commonwealth Blvd., Tallahassee 32399

**Florida Department of State, Division of Historic Resources**, Florida State Library, R.A. Gray Building, Tallahassee 32301

If you want to learn more about Florida's history, you're encouraged to contact or perhaps join the Florida Historical Society, Roesch House, 1320 Highland Ave., Melbourne 32935. (321)-254-9855.

Your community should also have a local historical society or museum, and your library should have historical material at its reference desk. Your town hall, county courthouse or schools should also have staffers familiar with local history.

*Sources*

Q: Where did you find all this stuff?
A: Here's a list of each question and its source or sources.

**1. Strange Florida**

1. (South Florida) *Sun-Sentinel*
2. *Palm Beach Post*
3. (South Florida) *Sun-Sentinel*
4. *Palm Beach Post*
5. *Palm Beach Post*
6. *Palm Beach Post*
7. Apalachicola Bay Chamber of Commerce
8. Calamity Calender
9. Associated Press
10. *Palm Beach Evening Times*
11. *Palm Beach Post*
12. *The Tropical Sun*
13. (South Florida) *Sun-Sentinel*
14. (South Florida) *Sun-Sentinel*
15. *Palm Beach Post*
16. *Palm Beach Post*
17. *Boone's Florida Historical Markers and Sites;* (South Florida) *Sun Sentinel*
18. Associated Press
19. *Florida Almanac*
20. *Palm Beach Post*
21. *Lakeland Ledger*
22. *Dallas Morning News*
23. Stoughton, Gertrude, *Tarpon Springs, the Early Years,* 1992, Tarpon Springs, Tarpon Springs Area Historical Society
24. Florida Department of Natural Resources; *Palm Beach Post*

25. (South Florida) *Sun-Sentinel*
26. *Florida Keys Keynoter*
27. *The Republic* newspaper, Key Largo
28. *Boone's Florida Historical Markers and Sites*
29. *Palm Beach Post*
30. *Boone's Florida Historical Markers and Sites*
31. *WPA Guide to Florida*
32. *WPA Guide to Florida*
33. *WPA Guide to Florida*
34. *Florida Vacation Guide*
35. *WPA Guide to Florida*
36. *Palm Beach Post*
37. *WPA Guide to Florida*
38. Associated Press
39. (South Florida) *Sun-Sentinel*
40. *Florida Times Union*
41. *Palm Beach Post*
42. (South Florida) *Sun-Sentinel*
43. Fuller, John Grant, *The Ghost of Flight 401, 1976,* New York: Berkley Publishing Group
44. *Palm Beach Post*
45. Greater South Brevard C. of C.
46. *Palm Beach Post*
47. Dale, James David, *An Eccentric Guide to the United States, 1977,* New York, Berkley Publishing Group
48. *Palm Beach Post*
49. *Palm Beach Post*
50. *Palm Beach Post*
51. *Palm Beach Post*
52. *Palm Beach Post*
53. *Palm Beach Post*

54. Coral Castle
55. Tarpon Springs Chamber of
    Commerce

## 2. Superlatives and Firsts
1. U.S. Census
2. *Florida Statistical Abstract*
3. *Florida Statistical Abstract*
4. *Florida Handbook; Florida Almanac*
5. *Florida Almanac*
6. *Florida Statistical Abstract*
7. *Florida Statistical Abstract*
8. *Florida Statistical Abstract*
9. Florida Official Map
10. *World Almanac and Book of Facts;*
    *Florida Handbook*
11. *World Almanac and Book of Facts*
12. *Palm Beach Post*
13. *Palm Beach Post*
14. *Palm Beach Post*
15. *Palm Beach Post*
16. *Palm Beach Post; World Almanac*
17. *Palm Beach Post*
18. *Palm Beach Post*
19. *Miami Herald*
20. *St. Petersburg Times*
21. *Palm Beach Post*
22. Greater Miami and the Beaches
    Tourism Council; Greater Miami
    Convention and Visitors Bureau
23. *Boone's Florida Historical Markers*
    *and Sites*
24. *Dallas Morning News*
25. Panama City Beach and Area
    Official Visitors' Guide
26. Wekiva Falls Park
27. Florida Department of Natural
    Resources
28. City of Panama City Beach
29. McWhirter, Norris and Ross,
    *Guinness Book of World Records*, 1982,
    New York, Bantam Books
30. *Palm Beach Post*
31. Florida Fish and Wildlife Conservation
    Commision
32. Florida Fish and Wildlife Conservation
    Commision
33. *Palm Beach Post; New Orleans Times*
    *Picayune*
34. *Palm Beach Post*
35. *Palm Beach Post*
36. *Palm Beach Post*

37. *Palm Beach Post*
38. *Palm Beach Post; St. Petersburg Times;*
    *Associated Press*
39. *Boone's Florida Historical Markers*
    *and Sites*
40. Associated Press
41. Associated Press
42. *Palm Beach Post*
43. *Florida Handbook*
44. *Florida Handbook*
45. *Florida Handbook*
46. *WPA Guide to Florida*
47. *Boone's Florida Historical Markers*
    *and Sites*
48. Kane, Joseph Nathan, *Famous First*
    *Facts*, 1981, New York, H.W. Wilson
49. *Florida Handbook; New York Times*
50. *Famous First Facts*
51. Florida Department of Natural
    Resources
52. *Famous First Facts*
53. Sea World

## 3. What's In a Name?
1. Florida Official Map
2. Florida Official Map
3. Florida Official Map
4. Florida Official Map
5. Florida Official Map
6. Florida Official Map
7. Florida Official Map
8. Morris, Allen Covington, *Florida*
    *Place Names*, 1974, Coral Gables,
    University of Miami Press
9. Florida Official Map; *Hammond*
    *World Atlas*
10. Florida Official Map; *Hammond*
    *World Atlas*
11. Florida Official Map; *Hammond*
    *World Atlas*
12. Florida Official Map
13. American Automobile Association
14. Florida Official Map
15. Florida Official Map
16. *Florida Almanac*
17. Florida Official Map
18. Florida Official Map
19. *Florida Almanac*
20. *Florida Handbook*
21. *Florida Handbook; Florida Almanac*
22. *Florida Almanac*
23. *Florida Handbook*

24. *Florida Handbook*
25. Florida Official Map; *A History of Florida*
26. *Florida Almanac*
27. Florida Official Map
28. *Florida Almanac*
29. Florida Official Map
30. *Florida Almanac*
31. *Florida Almanac*
32. Central Florida Community College, Ocala
33. *Florida Handbook*
34. *Florida Handbook; World Almanac and Book of Facts*
35. *Florida Handbook*
36. *Florida Handbook*
37. *Florida Handbook; Boone's Florida Historical Markers and Sites*
38. *Miami News*
39. *Florida Handbook; A History of Florida*
40. *Florida Place Names*
41. *Palm Beach Post*
42. *Miami Herald*
43. *Florida Place Names*
44. Jupiter historian Bessie Wilson DuBois
45. Jupiter historian Bessie Wilson DuBois
46. Boca Raton Historical Society
47. South Palm Beach County historian Mary Linehan
48. *Miami, The Way We Were*
49. Polk County Historical Society
50. *Boone's Florida Historical Markers and Sites*
51. Southern Living
52. *Florida Almanac; A History of Florida*
53. South Palm Beach County historian Mary Linehan
54. Florida Official Map
55. Florida Official Map
56. Indian River Chamber of Commerce
57. *Humm's Guide to the Florida Keys and Key West*
58. Key West Chamber of Commerce
59. *Florida Place Names*
60. Florida Keys Chamber of Commerce
61. *Humm's Guide to the Florida Keys and Key West*
62. Valparaiso-Niceville Chamber of Commerce
63. *Palatka Daily News*
64. *Miami News*
65. (South Florida) *Sun-Sentinel*
66. Marathon Chamber of Commerce
67. *Florida Place Names*
68. *WPA Guide to Florida*
69. *Boone's Florida Historical Markers and Sites*
70. Clearwater Chamber of Commerce
71. St. Petersburg area Chamber of Commerce
72. Broward County Historical Commission
73. *Florida Place Names*
74. St. Johns Historical Society
75. *Florida Place Names; Webster's Dictionary*
76. *Florida Place Names*
77. *Miami Herald*
78. *Boone's Florida Historical Markers and Sites*
79. *WPA Guide to Florida*
80. *Boone's Florida Historical Markers and Sites*
81. *Tampa Bay Relocation Guide*
82. Sarasota Convention and Visitors Bureau; American Automobile Association; *Dallas Morning News*
83. *Florida Handbook*
84. Greater Miami and the Beaches Tourism Council
85. *Florida Place Names*
86. *Florida Almanac*
87. *Florida Place Names*
88. Orlando Chamber of Commerce; Greater Miami Convention and Visitors Bureau
89. Jacksonville Chamber of Commerce
90. Ft. Lauderdale/Broward County Chamber of Commerce
91. Martin Chamber of Commerce
92. Cocoa Beach Area Chamber of Commerce
93. Destin Chamber of Commerce
94. Bay County Hotel and Restaurant Association
95. *Palm Beach Post*
96. *Miami, The Way We Were*
97. *Palm Beach Post*
98. *Florida Place Names*

99. *Florida Handbook*
100. Florida Official Map; State Road Department
101. Greater Miami and the Beaches Tourism Council
102. Florida's Turnpike
103. *Palm Beach Post*
104. *A History of Florida*

**4. Let's Go To The Map**
1. *Palm Beach Post*
2. *Florida Almanac*
3. *Florida Handbook*
4. *Florida Almanac*
5. *Florida Handbook*
6. *Florida Handbook; World Almanac and Book of Facts*
7. *Florida Handbook; World Almanac and Book of Facts*
8. *Florida Almanac; World Almanac and Book of Facts*
9. Florida Official Map
10. *Florida Almanac*
11. Florida Official Map; *Hammond World Atlas*
12. Florida Official Map; *Hammond World Atlas*
13. Florida Official Map; *Hammond World Atlas*
14. Florida Official Map; *Hammond World Atlas*
15. Florida Official Map; (Fort Lauderdale) *Sun-Sentinel*
16. *Florida Keys Keynoter*
17. *Florida Almanac*
18. Florida's Turnpike; Florida Official Map
19. Florida's Turnpike
20. Florida's Turnpike
21. American Automobile Association; *Dallas Morning News*
22. Florida Official Map
23. U.S. Department of Transportation
24. American Automobile Association
25. University of Florida
26. *Boone's Florida Historical Markers and Sites; WPA Guide to Florida*
27. Maitland-South Seminole Chamber of Commerce
28. *Palm Beach Post*
29. *Florida Almanac*
30. Florida Official Map

31. Florida Official Map
32. *Florida Handbook*
33. *Florida Handbook*
34. *Boone's Florida Historical Markers and Sites*
35. *Florida Handbook*
36. *Florida Handbook*
37. Jacksonville Chamber of Commerce
38. *Florida Almanac*
39. *A History of Florida*
40. Associated Press
41. *Miami Herald*
42. *Miami News*
43. *Florida Place Names*
44. Okeechobee Historical Society

**5. Business and Tourism**
1. *Palm Beach Post*
2. *A History of Florida*
3. *Florida Statistical Abstract; Florida Almanac*
4. *Florida Statistical Abstract; Florida Almanac*
5. Greater Miami Convention and Visitors Bureau
6. *Palm Beach Post*
7. Ormond Beach Chamber of Commerce
8. (South Florida) *Sun-Sentinel*
9. Sanibel/Captiva Islands Chamber of Commerce
10. *Palm Beach Post*
11. Miami Convention and Visitors Bureau
12. Walt Disney World; Mouseplanet.com
13. Walt Disney World
14. Walt Disney World
15. Walt Disney World
16. Walt Disney World
17. Walt Disney World
18. Walt Disney World
19. Walt Disney World
20. Walt Disney World; U.S. Census
21. Associated Press
22. Orlando/Orange County Covention & Visitors Bureau; Las Vegas Convention and Visitors Authority
23. Orlando/Orange County Covention & Visitors Bureau
24. Orlando/Orange County Covention & Visitors Bureau
25. *Dallas Morning News*

26. *Palm Beach Post*
27. *Palm Beach Post*
28. *WPA Guide to Florida; Florida Place Names*
29. Florida Department of Natural Resources
30. *An Eccentric Guide to the United States*
31. St. Augustine and St. Johns County Chamber of Commerce
32. American Automobile Association
33. (South Florida) *Sun-Sentinel*
34. Bok Tower; Winter Haven Area Chamber of Commerce
35. *Palm Beach Post*
36. American Automobile Association
37. *Palm Beach Post*
38. *Boone's Florida Historical Markers and Sites*
39. *Palm Beach Post*
40. *Boone's Florida Historical Markers and Sites*
41. *Boone's Florida Historical Markers and Sites*
42. Miami Convention and Visitors Bureau; Coconut Grove Arts Festival
43. Miami Convention and Visitors Bureau
44. *Miami Herald*
45. *New York Times*
46. *Florida Handbook*
47. Orlando/Orange County Covention & Visitors Bureau
48. *Boone's Florida Historical Markers and Sites*
49. Downtown Miami Development Authority
50. Port of Miami
51. *Traveler's Guide to Major U.S. Airports*
52. *Palm Beach Post*
53. (South Florida) *Sun-Sentinel*
54. Florida Thoroughbred Breeders and Owners Association
55. Florida Thoroughbred Breeders and Owners Association
56. *Palm Beach Post*
57. *Humm's Guide to the Florida Keys and Key West*
58. (South Florida) *Sun-Sentinel*
59. Burger King Corporation
60. Orlando/Orange County Covention & Visitors Bureau
61. Associated Press
62. *Humm's Guide to the Florida Keys and Key West*
63. Florida Department of Agriculture and Consumer Services
64. Florida Citrus Mutual
65. Florida Citrus Mutual
66. Florida Citrus Mutual
67. Florida Citrus Mutual
68. Florida Department of Natural Resources
69. Florida Sugar Cane League
70. U.S. Sugar
71. U.S. Sugar
72. U.S. Sugar
73. U.S. Sugar
74. Greater Miami Convention and Visitors Bureau; *Palm Beach Post*
75. *Florida Almanac*
76. Florida Forest Festival, Perry
77. *WPA Guide to Florida*
78. Ybor City Chamber of Commerce
79. Florida Keys & Key West Visitors Bureau
80. *Palm Beach Post*
81. Florida Cattleman's Association
82. Florida Department of Agriculture and Consumer Services
83. Florida Department of Agriculture and Consumer Services
84. (South Florida) *Sun-Sentinel*
85. Florida Department of Agriculture and Consumer Services
86. *Boone's Florida Historical Markers and Sites*
87. Winter Haven Area Chamber of Commerce
88. Winter Haven Area Chamber of Commerce
89. *Boone's Florida Historical Markers and Sites*

## 6. Sports
1. *Tampa Bay Metro Magazine*
2. *Florida Almanac*
3. Dr. Richard Crepeau, University of Central Florida
4. *Panama City News Herald*
5. Dr. Richard Crepeau, University of Central Florida
6. *Boone's Florida Historical Markers and Sites*
7. *Palm Beach Post*
8. Dr. Richard Crepeau, University of Central Florida; *World Almanac and*

Book of Facts; Miami Herald
9. University of Miami
10. Palm Beach Post; Tampa Bay Devil Rays
11. Palm Beach Post
12. (South Florida) Sun-Sentinel, Miami Herald
13. Parade Magazine
14. (South Florida) Sun-Sentinel
15. Palm Beach Post
16. Florida Almanac
17. World Almanac and Book of Facts; Palm Beach Post; Associated Press
18. University of Florida
19. Proctor, Samuel, Gator History, 1986, Gainesville, South Star Publishing
20. University of Florida
21. Gator History
22. Palm Beach Post
23. University of Florida
24. University of Florida
25. University of Florida
26. Palm Beach Post
27. World Almanac and Book of Facts
28. Miami News
29. NCAA
30. University of Miami
31. University of Miami; Palm Beach Post
32. Palm Beach Post
33. Palm Beach Post
34. Famous First Facts
35. Palm Beach Post
36. Dolphins '72 yearbook
37. Florida Official Map
38. Palm Beach Post; Sports Illustrated 1992 Sports Almanac, 1991, New York, Time Inc. Magazine Company
39. Tampa Bay Buccaneers
40. Florida Almanac
41. South Florida Sun-Sentinel
42. Neft, David S., Sports Encyclopedia: Pro Football, 1974, New York, Grosset & Dunlap
43. Tampa Bay Relocation Guide
44. Miami Herald
45. Palm Beach Post
46. Palm Beach Post
47. St. Petersburg Historical Society
48. World Almanac and Book of Facts; Palm Beach Post
49. Florida Almanac

50. National Golf Foundation
51. National Golf Foundation
52. National Golf Foundation
53. National Golf Foundation
54. Sarasota Convention and Visitors Bureau
55. Greater Miami Convention and Visitors Bureau
56. Florida's Past
57. World Almanac and Book of Facts
58. Greater Miami and the Beaches Tourism Council
59. Palm Beach Post
60. Palm Beach Post
61. Palm Beach Post
62. Humm's Guide to the Florida Keys and Key West
63. Palm Beach Post
64. Jacksonville and Beaches Convention and Visitors Bureau
65. Associated Press
66. International Diving Museum
67. Winter Haven Area Chamber of Commerce
68. Southern Living
69. Humm's Guide to the Florida Keys and Key West
70. (South Florida) Sun-Sentinel
71. (South Florida) Sun-Sentinel
72. Sebring Historical Society
73. American Automobile Association
74. NASCAR
75. WPA Guide to Florida; Palm Beach Post
76. Palm Beach Post
77. Palm Beach Post
78. Palm Beach Post
79. Palm Beach Post
80. Palm Beach Post
81. Palm Beach Post
82. Palm Beach Post

## 7. Let Me Entertain You

1. Palm Beach Post
2. Palm Beach Post
3. Palm Beach Post
4. Florida Keys & Key West Visitors Bureau
5. Florida Keys & Key West Visitors Bureau
6. Palm Beach Post
7. New York Times

8. (South Florida) *Sun-Sentinel*
9. *Palm Beach Post*
10. *Palm Beach Post*
11. *Palm Beach Post*
12. *Palm Beach Post*
13. *Palm Beach Post*
14. (South Florida) *Sun-Sentinel*
15. Greater Miami and the Beaches Tourism Council
16. *Southern Living*
17. (South Florida) *Sun-Sentinel*
18. (South Florida) *Sun-Sentinel;* Nite, Norm N., *Rock On*, 1989, New York, Harper Row
19. (South Florida) *Sun-Sentinel; Rock On*
20. Zimmer, Dave, *Crosby, Stills and Nash: the authorized biography*, 1984, New York, St. Martin's Press
21. *Palm Beach Post*
22. Stambler, Irwin, *Encyclopedia of Pop, Rock & Soul*, 1989, New York, St. Martin's Press
23. (South Florida) *Sun-Sentinel; Orlando Sentinel*
24. Roxon, Lillian, *Rock Encyclopedia*, 1969, New York, Grosset & Dunlap Publishers
25. *Miami Herald*
26. *Palm Beach Post*
27. (South Florida) *Sun-Sentinel*

**8. People**
1. *Boone's Florida Historical Markers and Sites;* Florida Keys Chamber of Commerce
2. McLendon, James, *Papa: Hemingway in Key West*, 1990, Miami, E.A. Seamann Publishing
3. *Papa: Hemingway in Key West*
4. (South Florida) *Sun-Sentinel*
5. (South Florida) *Sun-Sentinel*
6. *Palm Beach Post*
7. *Palm Beach Post*
8. *Palm Beach Post*
9. *Palm Beach Post*
.0. *Palm Beach Post*
.1. Proby. Kathryn Hall, *Audubon in Florida*, 1973, Coral Gables, University of Miami Press
.2. Salvador Dali Museum; *Florida Almanac;* (South Florida) *Sun-Sentinel*
.3. (South Florida) *Sun-Sentinel*

14. *Palm Beach Post*
15. *Palm Beach Post*
16. *Palm Beach Post*
17. *Palm Beach Post*
18. *Palm Beach Post*
19. (South Florida) *Sun-Sentinel*
20. *Florida Almanac*
21. *Florida Almanac*
22. *Palm Beach Post*
23. *Miami News;* Lisa Merkin & Eric Frankel, *Trivial Conquest*, 1984, New York, Avon Books
24. *Miami News*
25. (South Florida) *Sun-Sentinel*
26. *Miami News*
27. Greater Miami Convention and Visitors Bureau; *World Almanac and Book of Facts*
28. (South Florida) *Sun-Sentinel*
29. *Palm Beach Post*
30. Palatka Daily News; *Boone's Florida Historical Markers and Sites*
31. *Palm Beach Post*
32. (South Florida) *Sun-Sentinel*
33. (South Florida) *Sun-Sentinel; Palm Beach Post; Miami Herald*
34. *WPA Guide to Florida*
35. *WPA Guide to Florida*
36. *Glimpses of South Florida History*
37. *Palm Beach Post*
38. *Boone's Florida Historical Markers and Sites*
39. *Boone's Florida Historical Markers and Sites*
40. *Boone's Florida Historical Markers and Sites*
41. Sarasota Convention and Visitors Bureau
42. *Miami, The Way We Were*
43. Edison Winter Home, *Boone's Florida Historical Markers and Sites*, American Automobile Association
44. *The Everglades: River of Grass; WPA Guide to Florida*
45. *Miami Herald*
46. *Palm Beach Post*
47. *Miami News*
48. David Wallechinsky and Irving Wallace, *People's Almanac #2*, 1978, New York, Bantam Books; *Miami News*
49. *Florida Place Names*
50. (South Florida) *Sun-Sentinel*

51. *Palm Beach Post*
52. *New York Times;* Gene Miller with Barbara Jane Mackle, *Eighty-Three Hours to Dawn,* 1971, New York, Bantam Books
53. *WPA Guide to Florida*
54. *Boone's Florida Historical Markers and Sites*
55. *Florida Almanac;* Florida Dept. of Veterans' Affairs
56. *The Florida Bicentennial Trail: A Heritage Revisited*
57. Organization of American States

**9. Politics**

1. *Florida Handbook*
2. *A History of Florida*
3. *A History of Florida*
4. Florida Department of State
5. Florida Department of State
6. *Florida Handbook*
7. *Florida Handbook*
8. *The Everglades: River of Grass*
9. *Miami, The Way We Were*
10. *Florida Handbook*
11. *New York Times; World Almanac and Book of Facts*
12. *Florida Handbook*
13. *Florida Handbook*
14. *New York Times*
15. *Palm Beach Post*
16. *Palm Beach Post*
17. *Palm Beach Post*
18. *Tallahassee Democrat*
19. *Palm Beach Post; World Almanac and Book of Facts*
20. Museum of Florida History; Johnston, Otto, *Information Please Almanac,* 1985. Boston, Houghton Miflin Company
21. *Palm Beach Post; Miami News*
22. *Palm Beach Post*
23. *Palm Beach Post*
24. *New York Times*
25. *Palm Beach Post*
26. *Palm Beach Post*
27. *Palm Beach Post*
28. *Florida Handbook*
29. *Florida Handbook*
30. *Florida Handbook*
31. U.S. Sen. Bob Graham (D-Fla.)
32. *Florida Handbook*
33. (South Florida) *Sun-Sentinel*
34. *Dallas Morning News*
35. *Palm Beach Post*
36. *New York Times*
37. *New York Times*
38. *Miami News*
39. *Palm Beach Post*
40. *Palm Beach Post*
41. *Palm Beach Post*
42. *Information Please Almanac*
43. *Florida Almanac*
44. *New York Times*
45. Bernstein, Carl, and Bob Woodward, *The Final Days,* 1976, New York, Simon & Schuster
46. *Palm Beach Post*
47. *Florida Almanac*
48. *Florida Almanac*
49. *Florida Almanac*
50. *Palm Beach Post*
51. Florida House
52. *Florida Handbook; World Almanac*

**10. Animal, Vegetable, Mineral**

1. *Palm Beach Post*
2. *Palm Beach Post*
3. *Palm Beach Post*
4. *Palm Beach Post*
5. *Palm Beach Post*
6. *Florida Keys Keynoter*
7. *Palm Beach Post*
8. *Palm Beach Post*
9. Greater Venice Area Chamber of Commerce
10. *Florida Handbook*
11. *Palm Beach Post*
12. *Webster's Dictionary*
13. Anderson, Robert, *Guide to Florida Alligators and Crocodiles,* 1985, Oviedo, Mickler's Floridiana
14. *Miami Herald*
15. *Palm Beach Post; Florida Handbook*
16. *Palm Beach Post*
17. *Southern Living*
18. *Palm Beach Post*
19. *Florida Handbook; Florida Cowman*
20. *Palm Beach Post*
21. *Palm Beach Post*
22. Associated Press
23. *Palm Beach Post*
24. *Florida Almanac*
25. *Florida Almanac*
26. Calamity Calendar
27. *Palm Beach Post*

28. *Palm Beach Post*
29. Greater Miami and the Beaches Tourism Council
30. *Florida Handbook*
31. *Palm Beach Post*
32. *Humm's Guide to the Florida Keys and Key West*
33. Florida Keys & Key West Visitors Bureau
34. *Palm Beach Post*
35. Lake Placid Chamber of Commerce
36. Sarasota Convention and Visitors Bureau
37. American Automobile Association; *Boone's Florida Historical Markers and Sites*
38. *Palm Beach Post*
39. University of Florida
40. National Park Service
41. Palm Beach County Artificial Reef Committee
42. *Famous First Facts; Florida Almanac*
43. U.S. Dept. of Interior
44. *Palm Beach Post*
45. Audubon Society
46. *Palm Beach Post*

**11. Science, Weather and the Environment**

1. *The Florida Bicentennial Trail: A Heritage Revisited*
2. *Palm Beach Post*
3. *Palm Beach Post*
4. Cape Coral Utilities
5. Cocoa Beach Area Chamber of Commerce
6. *Florida Handbook*
7. *Florida Almanac*
8. (South Florida) *Sun-Sentinel*
9. *Miami Herald*
10. *Florida Almanac*
11. *Florida Handbook*
12. University of Florida
13. South Florida Water Management District
14. *Palm Beach Post*
15. *Florida Handbook*
16. *Water Resources Atlas of Florida*
17. *Miami, The Way We Were*
18. *Palm Beach Post*
19. *Miami, The Way We Were; WPA Guide to Florida*
20. *Water Resources Atlas of Florida*

21. *Palm Beach Post*
22. *Florida Almanac*; U.S. Department of Commerce
23. *Florida Handbook*
24. *Florida Almanac; Palm Beach Post*
25. *WPA Guide to Florida*
26. *Palm Beach Post; Florida Almanac*
27. *Palm Beach Post*
28. *Famous First Facts*
29. *Palmetto Country*
30. Florida Department of Natural Resources
31. Florida Official Map
32. *Palm Beach Post*
33. *Palm Beach Post*
34. *Florida: From Indian Trail to Space Age*
35. (South Florida) *Sun-Sentinel*
36. *Boone's Florida Historical Markers and Sites*
37. Greater Venice Area Chamber of Commerce
38. *Florida Keys Keynoter*

**12. History: Age of Exploration** (to 1776)

1. *Florida Handbook*
2. Florida Department of State
3. *A History of Florida*
4. *A History of Florida*
5. *Palm Beach Post*
6. *Boone's Florida Historical Markers and Sites*
7. *Florida Handbook*
8. *Boone's Florida Historical Markers and Sites*; Douglas, Marjory Stoneman, *Florida: The Long Frontier*, 1967, New York, Harper & Row
9. *A History of Florida*
10. *Boone's Florida Historical Markers and Sites*
11. Tampa/Hillsborough Convention and Visitors Association
12. *Palm Beach Post*
13. *Florida Handbook*
14. *Boone's Florida Historical Markers and Sites*
15. *Boone's Florida Historical Markers and Sites*
16. *A History of Florida; World Almanac and Book of Facts*
17. *Florida Almanac*
18. *Boone's Florida Historical Markers*

and Sites
19. *A History of Florida; The Florida Bicentennial Trail: A Heritage Revisited*
20. *Tampa Tribune*
21. Florida Department of State
22. *Palm Beach Post*
23. *Boone's Florida Historical Markers and Sites*
24. Associated Press
25. (South Florida) *Sun-Sentinel*
26. *Tampa Bay MetroMagazine*
27. *Palm Beach Post*
28. *Boone's Florida Historical Markers and Sites; Florida: The Long Frontier*
29. Florida Department of Natural Resources
30. Florida Department of State
31. *Palm Beach Post*
32. *Florida Almanac*
33. *A History of Florida*
34. *Florida's Past*
35. *Boone's Florida Historical Markers Sites*; Rolle, Denys, *Humble Petition,* 1977, Gainesville, University Press of Florida
36. Florida Department of State; (Fort Lauderdale) *Sun-Sentinel*
37. *A History of Florida*

## 13. History: Redcoats to Rebellion
### (1776-1861)
1. *Born of the Sun*
2. (South Florida) *Sun-Sentinel*
3. (South Florida) *Sun-Sentinel*
4. *A History of Florida*
5. *WPA Guide to Florida*; Florida Historical Society
6. *Florida Handbook*
7. *WPA Guide to Florida*
8. Florida Historical Society
9. *A History of Florida*
10. *A History of Florida*; Smith, Joseph Burkholder, *The Plot to Steal Florida,* 1983, New York, Arbor House
11. Florida Department of State
12. *Florida Handbook*
13. Palace Saloon, Fernandina Beach; *Ocala Star-Banner*
14. Palace Saloon
15. *Boone's Florida Historical Markers and Sites*
16. Florida Department of Natural

Resources; *A History of Florida*
17. *A History of Florida*
18. *WPA Guide to Florida*
19. *Boone's Florida Historical Markers and Sites*
20. *Boone's Florida Historical Markers and Sites*
21. *Boone's Florida Historical Markers and Sites*
22. *Florida Handbook*
23. *Boone's Florida Historical Markers and Sites*
24. *Boone's Florida Historical Markers and Sites*
25. *Boone's Florida Historical Markers and Sites*
26. *History of the Second Seminole War;* Florida Department of Natural Resources
27. (South Florida) *Sun-Sentinel*
28. Florida Department of Natural Resources
29. (South Florida) *Sun-Sentinel*
30. *Boone's Florida Historical Markers and Sites*
31. *Palm Beach Post; Boone's Florida Historical Markers and Sites*
32. American Automobile Association; *Boone's Florida Historical Markers and Sites*
33. *Palm Beach Post*
34. *Palm Beach Post*
35. Florida Department of Natural Resources
36. *WPA Guide to Florida*
37. *The Everglades: River of Grass*
38. *Boone's Florida Historical Markers and Sites; Florida Bicentennial Trail: A Heritage Revisited*
39. *Florida's Past*
40. *Palatka Daily News*
41. *A History of Florida*
42. Florida Department of Natural Resources
43. Florida Department of State
44. University of Florida
45. *Boone's Florida Historical Markers and Sites*
46. *Boone's Florida Historical Markers and Sites*

## 14. History: Civil War in Florida
### (1861-1865)

1. *Florida Handbook*
2. Florida Department of State
3. *Florida's Past*
4. Liberty County Chamber of Commerce; *North Florida Living*
5. *Florida Handbook*
6. *Florida Handbook*
7. *Florida Handbook*
8. *Boone's Florida Historical Markers and Sites; World Book Encyclopedia,* 1992, Chicago, World Book, Inc.
9. (South Florida) *Sun-Sentinel*
10. Jupiter historian Bessie Wilson DuBois
11. *Palm Beach Post*
12. *A History of Florida*
13. *A History of Florida*
14. Florida Department of Natural Resources
15. Virginia Historical Society
16. *WPA Guide to Florida;* American Automobile Association
17. *WPA Guide to Florida*
18. *Boone's Florida Historical Markers and Sites; World Book*
19. *Florida Handbook*
20. Florida Department of Natural Resources
21. *Florida Handbook*
22. *Florida's Past*
23. *Florida Handbook*
24. *Florida's Past;* (South Florida) *Sun-Sentinel; Palm Beach Post*
25. *Palm Beach Post*
26. *Florida's Past; A History of Florida*
27. Associated Press; *World Book*
28. *Florida Handbook*
29. *Boone's Florida Historical Markers and Sites*
30. *Union Times* reenactors' newsletter
31. *Palm Beach Post*

## 15. History: The Boom Years (1865-1941)

1. *Palm Beach Post*
2. *A History of Florida*
3. *New York Times; Boone's Florida Historical Markers and Sites*
4. *Yesterday's Palm Beach*
5. Barnett Bank
6. *A History of Florida*
7. Florida Department of State
8. *WPA Guide to Florida*
9. *Lee County Centennial*
10. *Palm Beach Post*
11. St. Petersburg Area Chamber of Commerce
12. (South Florida) *Sun-Sentinel*
13. DeSoto County Chamber of Commerce
14. *New York Times*
15. (South Florida) *Sun-Sentinel*
16. *Boone's Florida Historical Markers and Sites*
17. Organization of American States
18. Organization of American States
19. *Boone's Florida Historical Markers and Sites*
20. *A History of Florida; Glimpses of South Florida History*
21. *Dallas Morning News, Palm Beach Post*
22. *Palmetto Country*
23. *Tropical Sun*
24. *Florida Handbook; Miami, The Way We Were*
25. *Miami, The Way We Were*
26. *Boone's Florida Historical Markers and Sites*
27. *Boone's Florida Historical Markers and Sites*
28. *Boone's Florida Historical Markers and Sites*
29. (South Florida) *Sun-Sentinel; Yesterday's Palm Beach*
30. Jacksonville Chamber of Commerce
31. University of Florida
32. University of Florida
33. University of Florida
34. (South Florida) *Sun-Sentinel*
35. *Boone's Florida Historical Markers and Sites*
36. *Boone's Florida Historical Markers and Sites;* Marathon Chamber of Commerce
37. *Boone's Florida Historical Markers and Sites;* Marathon Chamber of Commerce
38. *Miami, The Way We Were*
39. *Boone's Florida Historical Markers and Sites; Miami, The Way We Were*
40. *Boone's Florida Historical Markers and Sites*

41. *Florida Handbook*
42. *New York Times*
43. *Panama City News Herald*
44. *Famous First Facts*
45. *Panama City News Herald*
46. Beaches Area Historical Society
47. *Florida Handbook*
48. *A History of Florida*
49. Greater Miami Convention and Visitors Bureau
50. *Palm Beach Evening Times*
51. *Boone's Florida Historical Markers and Sites*
52. *Palm Beach Post; Miami Herald*
53. *Palm Beach Post*
54. *Palm Beach Evening Times*
55. *Boone's Florida Historical Markers and Sites;* Valparaiso-Niceville Chamber of Commerce
56. *WPA Guide to Florida*
57. *New York Times*
58. Florida Department of Corrections
59. Florida Department of Corrections; Florida Sheriff's Association
60. Florida Department of Corrections
61. (South Florida) *Sun-Sentinel*
62. *New York Times*
63. (South Florida) *Sun-Sentinel*
64. *Boone's Florida Historical Markers and Sites*
65. *Palm Beach Post*
66. *New York Times*
67. Greater Miami Convention and Visitors Bureau; *The People's Almanac*
68. Jahoda, Gloria, *River of the Golden Ibis*, 1973, New York, Holt, Rinehart & Winston
69. *WPA Guide to Florida; A History of Florida*
70. *LaBelle Leader*
71. *Boone's Florida Historical Markers and Sites*
72. *Glimpses of South Florida History*
73. *Boone's Florida Historical Markers and Sites*
74. *Palm Beach Post*
75. St. Petersburg Historical Society
76. *Boone's Florida Historical Markers and Sites*
77. *New York Times*
78. *Florida's Past*
79. Florida Historical Society
80. McGoun, William E., *A Biographical History of Broward County*, 1975, Miami, Miami Herald Publishing
81. *Boone's Florida Historical Markers and Sites*
82. *Miami, The Way We Were*
83. *Boone's Florida Historical Markers and Sites; Palm Beach Post*
84. *Palm Beach Post*
85. *Miami, The Way We Were*
86. *Palm Beach Post;* (Fort Lauderdale) *Sun-Sentinel; Miami, The Way We Were*
87. *Orlando Sentinel*
88. *Boone's Florida Historical Markers and Sites*

## 16. History: Modern Florida (Since 1941)

1. *Florida Handbook, A History of Florida*
2. *LIFE* magazine
3. *Boone's Florida Historical Markers and Sites*
4. *Palm Beach Post*
5. *Palm Beach Post*
6. Valparaiso-Niceville Chamber of Commerce
7. *A History of Florida;* Beaches Area Historical Society
8. (South Florida) *Sun-Sentinel*
9. Terraine, John, *The U-Boat Wars*, 1989, New York, Putnam Berkley Group; (South Florida) *Sun-Sentinel*
10. *Palm Beach Post*
11. *Florida Times Union*
12. *Boone's Florida Historical Markers and Sites*
13. *Gator History*
14. University of Florida
15. University of Florida
16. *A History of Florida*
17. *Florida Handbook*
18. *Palm Beach Post*
19. *Miami News*
20. *Palm Beach Post*
21. *Boone's Florida Historical Markers and Sites; Information Please Almanac; Palm Beach Post*
22. *Famous First Facts*
23. *Florida Handbook*
24. (South Florida) *Sun-Sentinel*
25. *A History of Florida; Florida Handbook; Palm Beach Post*

26. *Palm Beach Post*
27. *Palm Beach Post*
28. *Famous First Facts*
29. *Florida Handbook*
30. *World Almanac and Book of Facts*
31. *Boone's Florida Historical Markers and Sites*
32. *Facts on File*
33. (South Florida) *Sun-Sentinel*
34. *Florida Handbook*
35. *Boone's Florida Historical Markers and Sites; Palm Beach Post*
36. Florida Historical Society, *Miami News*
37. *Dallas Morning News*
38. *Miami Herald*
39. *Palm Beach Post*
40. *Boone's Florida Historical Markers and Sites*
41. *Palm Beach Post*
42. *Palm Beach Post*
43. *Palm Beach Post*
44. (South Florida) *Sun-Sentinel*
45. *Florida Almanac*
46. *Florida Almanac*
47. *Orlando Sentinel, Palm Beach Post*
48. *New York Times*
49. *Facts on File*
50. WCPX-TV
51. *Florida Almanac*
52. *Palm Beach Post*
53. *Florida Almanac*
54. (South Florida) *Sun-Sentinel*
55. St. Petersburg Historical Society
56. Vizcaya
57. (South Florida) *Sun-Sentinel*
58. *Palm Beach Post*
59. *Palm Beach Post*
60. U.S. Census
61. *Palm Beach Post*
62. *Florida Statistical Abstract*
63. *Palm Beach Post*
64. U.S. Census
65. U.S. Census
66. *Palm Beach Post*
67. *Palm Beach Post*
68. *Palm Beach Post*
69. *Palm Beach Post*
70. *Palm Beach Post*

**17. Florida Stew**
1. *Born of the Sun*
2. *Palm Beach Post*
3. Florida Department of State
4. Florida Department of State
5. Florida Department of State
6. Florida Department of State
7. Florida Department of State
8. Florida Department of State
9. Florida Department of State
10. Florida Department of Natural Resources
11. *Palm Beach Post; Hammond World Atlas*
12. Florida Department of State
13. *Palm Beach Post*
14. *Palm Beach Post*; Florida Department of State
15. Florida Department of State
16. Florida Department of State
17. Florida Department of State
18. Florida Department of State
19. Florida Department of State
20. Florida Department of State
21. State of Florida University System
22. Florida Atlantic University
23. Florida Department of State
24. *Palm Beach Post*
25. *Guide to Fort Lauderdale;* University of Florida
26. *Palm Beach Post*
27. *World Almanac and Book of Facts*
28. *Palm Beach Post;*(South Florida) *Sun-Sentinel*
29. U.S. Drug Enforcement Administration
30. Union Correctional Institute
31. *Palm Beach Post*
32. *Palm Beach Post*
33. U.S. Department of Veterans Affairs
34. *Palm Beach Post*
35. *Palm Beach Post; American Jewish Year Book 1993*, Philadelphia, American Jewish Committee
36. Audit Bureau of Circulation
37. *Palm Beach Post*
38. *Palm Beach Post*
39. *Florida Almanac*
40. (South Florida) *Sun-Sentinel*
41. *Palm Beach Post*
42. *Dallas Morning News*
43. Greater Miami and the Beaches Tourism Council

44. Greater Miami and the Beaches
    Tourism Council
45. Greater Miami Convention and
    Visitors Bureau
46. *Palm Beach Post*
47. Greater Miami and the Beaches
    Tourism Council; *Miami Herald*
48. (South Florida) *Sun-Sentinel*
49. (South Florida) *Sun-Sentinel*
50. Greater Miami and the Beaches
    Tourism Council
51. Florida's Turnpike
52. Florida's Turnpike
53. *Florida Almanac*
54. Florida Department of State
55. *Playground Visitor*
56. Florida Official Map
57. *Palm Beach Post*
58. *Florida Almanac*
59. *Palm Beach Post*
60. *Florida Handbook*
61. *Calamity Calendar*; Canada News
62. *Palm Beach Post*
63. Greater Miami Convention and
    Visitors Bureau
64. *Florida Almanac*
65. *Palm Beach Post*; Florida Public Service
    Commission
66. (South Florida) *Sun-Sentinel*;
    Palace Saloon
67. (South Florida) *Sun-Sentinel*; *Sarasota
    Tribune*
68. *Palatka Daily News*
69. *Miami News*; *Boone's Florida
    Historical Markers and Sites*
70. *Miami Herald*
71. *Humm's Guide to the Florida Keys
    and Key West*
72. *Miami Herald*
73. Greater Miami Convention and
    Visitors Bureau
74. Greater Miami Convention and
    Visitors Bureau
75. Associated Press
76. *Florida Almanac*
77. *Florida Statistical Abstract*
78. *Florida Statistical Abstract*
79. Associated Press
80. *Miami Herald*
81. Division of Alcoholic Beverages and
    Tobacco
82. Greater Miami and the Beaches
    Tourism Council

# *Index*

Without an index, this is an entertainment book. With an index, it's a reference of sorts about Florida.

The index has been split into two parts. The first covers cities and the counties. The second, a general index, begins on page 24.

Because *Florida Fun Facts* is a collection of 1,001 questions and answers rather than a traditional book, written in prose form, we believed it would be easier for you if we gave not the page number, but the exact chapter and question for an item. For example, the entry **Bardin Booger 1.16** tells you to find a reference to the Bardin Booger in Chapter 1, Question 16.

Music: Caribbean 8.15-8.16, country 8.14, 17.67, rock 7.18-7.27
*Mutiny on the Bounty* (film), 5.33
Myakka River, 2.17
Myrtle Beach, S.C., 6.52
Mythology, 3.12, 3.75

**N**

Namath, Joe (athlete), 6.42
Napoleon, (SEE Bonaparte, Napoleon)
Nassau, Bahamas, 3.35
Nassau duchy (Germany), 3.35
National Aeronautics and Space Administration (NASA), 1.41, 11.2
National Association for the Advancement of Colored People (NAACP), 16.18
National Basketball Association (NBA), 6.49
National Collegiate Athletic Association (NCAA), 6.25, 6.48
*National Enquirer* (tabloid), 17.37
National Football League (NFL), 6.36-6.42, 6.46, 6.79, 6.81-6.82
National Golf Foundation, 6.51
National Hurricane Center, 11.21, 16.66
National parks, (SEE Parks, national)
Natural Bridge, Battle of, 14.20-14.21
Natural Resources, Florida Department of, 17.26
Navy, U.S.: 1.25, 1.38, 1.42, 5.36, 6.66, 13.20, air stations 5.36, 16.24, 17.39, Blue Angels 17.39, Cuban missile crisis 16.24, World War II 16.2
Nazi, 16.7
Nebraska, 2.11
Nebraska, University of, 6.27
"Negro Fort," 13.16
Nelson, Bill (politician, astronaut), 9.52
*Network* (film), 8.19
Nevada, 2.11, 16.60
New Deal, 15.84
New Jersey, 1.15, 4.29 sports 6.82
New Mexico, 2.11, 3.34
New Jerusalem, 1.48
New Orleans, 4.39, 6.41, 12.33
New River, 8.53, Stranahan 15.80
"New World", 2.39, 12.6, 12.20
New York, N.Y., 3.11, 4.7, 4.9, 4.13, 5.14, 5.37, 17.34, 17.73, personalities 15.64, sports 6.13, 6.42
New York (state), 3.35, 3.61, 5.3, sports 6.82, population 16.62

New York Giants (football), 6.82
New York Jets (football) 6.42, 6.82
New York Yankees (baseball), 6.13
*News/Sun-Sentinel* newspaper (Fort Lauderdale), 57.36
Newspaper: 5.79, 13.43, 15.50-15.51, 15.69, 16.55, 16.59, first 13.7, largest 57.36, tabloid 17.37
Nicaragua, 16.38
"Night 2,000 Died, The", (1928 hurricane) 4.41, 11.18
Nixon, Richard (president), 2.52, 9.42, 9.44-9.46, 17.75
Nobel Prize, 8.4
Nombre de Dios mission, 2.39
Norfolk, Va., 4.7
Noriega, Manuel (Panamian leader),16.63
North Atlantic Treaty Organization (NATO), 9.46
North Dakota, 2.11
North Florida: 4.1, 12.6, area code 17.65, earthquakes 11.24, hurricanes 11.16, politics 15.77, sugar 5.69
Nuclear: power plants 17.38, submarine 17.18
Nuclear war, 17.40, 17.58
Nude, 1.8
Numerology, 1.12

**O**

O'Neal, Patrick (actor), 16.13
Oakland, Calif., 3.10
Oakland Athletics (baseball), 6.11
Ocala National forest, 11.28
Odessa, Russia, 3.9
Ohio, 2.11, 3.10, 4.3, 6.82
Oil, 2.45, 8.34
Okeechobee Waterway, 4.30
Okefenokee Swamp, 11.31
Oklahoma, 13.33, 13.45
"Old Folks at Home" (state song), 17.10-17.11
Old Joe (alligator), 1.17
Old Spanish Trail, 4.26
O'Leno State Park, 3.69
Oliver, R.E. (state rep.), 15.77
Olympics, 8.32
Omaha, Neb., 6.9
Orange, 3.4, 3.31, 3.59, 5.64-5.66
Orange blossom (state flower), 17.8
Orange Bowl (stadium), 6.15, 6.26-6.27,

Poitier, Sidney (actor), 8.23
Police, 1.7, 6.8, 9.47, 15.87, 16.44-16.45
Polk, James K. (president), 3.17, 3.19
Ponce de León, Juan, 3.25, 10.19, 12.1-2.4
Pontiac, Mich, 6.41
Pope John Paul II, 16.56
Pork, 3.52
"Port", 3.2
Portland, Maine, 3.11
Post office, 2.20, 3.13
Postal Service, U.S., 4.43
Potatoes, 1.36, 15.47
Poverty level (in Florida), 17.79
Power plants, 17.38, 17.58
Preserves, national, 11.32
Presidents, U.S.: Adams 3.17,
  Buchanan 3.17, Bush 16.2, Calhoun
  3.24, Cleveland 3.17, Coolidge 15.49,
  Eisenhower 9.20, Grant 3.17, Harding
  17.75, Hoover 17.75, Jackson 3.34, 3.51,
  4.34, Jefferson 3.78, Johnson 17.75,
  Kennedy 9.39-9.41, 9.40, 17.40, Lincoln
  14.25, Madison 13.10, Monroe 3,17,
  13.14, Nixon 2.52, 9.42, 9.44-9.46, 17.75,
  Pierce 3.17, Polk 3.17, 3.19, Reagan 9.19,
  9.46-9.47, 16.13, 16.56. Roosevelt,
  Franklin 9.38, 15.86, Roosevelt,
  Theodore 15.19, Taylor 3.23, 13.33-13.34,
  Truman 9.20, 9.37, 11.34, 16.16,
  Washington 3.19, yacht 9.50
Presley, Elvis, (performer) 5.35, 8.13
Pretzel, 2.37
Princeton, N.J., 3.11
Privy, 16.10
Pro Player Stadium, 6.15, 6.41, 6.79
Professional Golfers Association
  (PGA), 6.55
Prohibition, 1.10, 15.54, 15.71-15.72
Protestant, 12.15
Providence, R.I., 3.11
*Providencia* (ship), 15.4
Pulitzer Prize, 5.34, 8.4, 8.6

**Q**
Quebec, 5.10
Quincy, Mass., 3.11

**R**
Radio, 8.26, 9.31, 15.51, 15.86
Radio Marti, 8.57
Railroad: 1.26, 1.35. 1.40, 3.49, 3.69,
  8.56, 15.5, 15.25-15.26, Celestial 3.103,

first 2.43, first cross-state, 14.6, Keys
  3.66, 15.36-15.37
Raleigh, N.C.. 3.10
Rain: 11.13, 11.16, 15.68, 16.43, in hurri-
  canes 11.16, 11.20, record 11.15
Rainy season, 11.13
Rally for Decency (1969), 7.19
Rattlesnake (community), 8.49
Rattlesnakes, 8.49
Rawlings, Marjorie Kinnan (writer),
  8.6-8.8
Raymond James Stadium, 6.41
Reagan, Ronald (president), 9.19,
  9.46-9.47, 16.13, 16.56
Real estate, 6.5, 15.67-15.68, 15.79-15.80,
  17.67
Reaver, J. Russell (folklore researcher),
  1.50
Reconstruction, 9.29
Red Brigade (Italian terrorist group),
  16.49
Red Cross Drug Store, 15.85
"Redcoats", (SEE British)
"Redneck Riviera", 3.95
Reefs, 2.18, 3.58, 10.41, 12.28, 17.71
Reggae, 7.25
"Reign of Terror" (French Revolution),
  13.22
Remington, Frederic, 15.23
Representatives, Florida, (SEE House
  of Representatives)
Representatives, U.S., (SEE House of
  Representatives)
Republican party, 9.20, 9.22, 9.25, 9.27,
  9.29, 9.42-9.43, 9.47
Reverse osmosis water treatment, 11.4
Revolution, U.S., 3.16, 3.22, 4.36,
  13.1-13.9, 13.22
Reynolds, Burt (performer), 6.45,
  8.17-8.18
Rhode Island, 2.16, 11.26, 13.8. 17.55
Rice, 10.3, 17.44
Richmond, Va., 14.15
Rickenbacker, Eddie (air pioneer), 5.48
Ride, Sally (first American woman in
  space), 16.51
Ringling, John (circus owner, pioneer),
  1.15, 1.20, 8.40-8.41
Ringling Brothers & Barnum and Bailey
  Circus, 5.41
Riots: Liberty City (Miami), 16.44-16.45
"River of Grass", 11.33
"River of May (Riviere de la Mai)",

### A FINAL NOTE TO THE READER:

**Q:** Who can help write the second edition of *Florida Fun Facts?*

**A:** You! We welcome your Florida trivia material. Unlike a certain game show, we do not require it to be in the form of a question. Please include a verifiable source or sources. Sorry, we can't compensate you for your entry, but we will list all contributors. Material is welcome from individuals or from groups such as tourism boards and chambers of commerce, historical societies and libraries, and local, state and federal agencies.

**Q:** Where should you write us?

**A:** Address correspondence to: *Florida Fun Facts,* c/o PINEAPPLE PRESS, INC., P.O. Box 3889, Sarasota, Florida 34230

**Q:** Do we thank you again for your interest?

**A:** You bet!

If you enjoyed reading this book, here are some other books from Pineapple Press on related topics. For a complete catalog, write to Pineapple Press, P.O. Box 3889, Sarasota, FL 34230 or call 1-800-PINEAPL (746-3275). Or visit our website at www.pineapplepress.com.

*The Book Lover's Guide to Florida* edited by Kevin McCarthy. Learn which authors lived in or wrote about a place in Florida, which books describe a place, and what important movies were made there in this exhaustive survey of writers, books, and literary sites. ISBN 1-56164-012-3 (hb); ISBN 1-56164-021-2 (pb)

*Hemingway's Key West* Second Edition by Stuart McIver. A vivid portrait that reveals details of the writer's life in the place he called home during his most productive years. This new edition has been updated to include a record of the author's exploits in Bimini and Cuba as well. ISBN 1-56164-241-X (pb)

*Marjory Stoneman Douglas: Voice of the River* by Marjory Stoneman Douglas with John Rothchild. The story of an illustrious, influential life told in a unique and spirited voice. Meet the woman who saved the Everglades from destruction while she crusaded for the rights of those with no voice of their own. ISBN 0-910923-33-7 (hb); ISBN 0-910923-94-9 (pb)

*The Florida Chronicles* by Stuart B. McIver. A series offering true-life sagas of the notable and notorious characters throughout history who have given Florida its distinctive flavor. **Volume 1**: *Dreamers, Schemers and Scalawags* ISBN 1-56164-155-3 (pb); **Volume 2**: *Murder in the Tropics* ISBN 1-56164-079-4 (hb); **Volume 3**: *Touched by the Sun* ISBN 1-56164-206-1 (hb)

*The Florida Keys* by John Viele. The trials and successes of the Keys pioneers are brought to life in this series, which recounts tales of early pioneer life and life at sea. **Volume 1**: *A History of the Pioneers* ISBN 1-56164-101-4 (hb); **Volume 2**: *True Stories of the Perilous Straits* ISBN 1-56164-179-0 (hb); **Volume 3**: *The Wreckers* ISBN 1-56164-219-3 (hb)

*Florida's Past* by Gene Burnett. Collected essays from Burnett's "Florida's Past" columns in *Florida Trend* magazine, plus some original writings not found elsewhere. Burnett's easygoing style and his sometimes surprising choice of topics make history good reading. **Volume 1** ISBN 1-56164-115-4 (pb); **Volume 2** ISBN 1-56164-139-1 (pb); **Volume 3** ISBN 1-56164-117-0 (pb)

*200 Quick Looks at Florida History* by James Clark. Here's the distilled version of Florida's 10,000 years of rich and varied history, from the arrival of the first natives to the annual arrival of the snowbirds. These history lessons are quick and painless. ISBN 1-56164-200-2 (pb)

*Florida's Finest Inns and Bed & Breakfasts* by Bruce Hunt. From warm and cozy country bed & breakfasts to elegant and historic hotels, author Bruce Hunt has composed the definitive guide to Florida's most quaint, romantic, and often eclectic lodgings. With photos and charming pen-and-ink drawings by the author. ISBN 1-56164-202-9 (pb)